The Creatures
of the
Great Garden

Siobhan McSwiggan

Copyright © 2023 Siobhan McSwiggan.

All rights reserved.

No part of this publication may be reproduced, distributed, or transmitted in any form or by any means, including photocopying, recording, or other electronic or mechanical methods, without the prior written permission of the publisher, except in the case of brief quotations embodied in critical reviews and certain other noncommercial uses permitted by copyright law.

ISBN:

DEDICATION

This book is dedicated to Jackie Sky (Marrot) who believed in it even when I didn't. Without her consistent encouragement it would have lived on my computer with so many other projects and never seen the light of day.

Also, to Jim and my three brilliant children who always supporting whatever hair brain scheme I come up with, for your constant love and encouragement.

Table of Contents

Acknowledgments vii

A Map of Wrest Park 1

Prologue 2

1. Freedom 5
2. The Evening Meeting 8
3. Spud and Radish 14
4. The visit to the Kitchen Garden 17
5. Manor farm 22
6. In the Kitchen Garden 25
7. The Great Fire 30
8. Screams of Terror 34
9. Dawn the next morning 36
10. Later that Day 40
11. Evening Meeting..45
12. The Evacuation 49
13. Father Squirrel..53
14. Brazil's New Home..55
15. The Next Morning...57
16. Mother Squirrels...60
17. Emergency meeting...64
18. Mother Squirrel returns home 69

19. The Divide Grows 72

20. The Harvest Party.. 75

21. Father Squirrel's Pain 76

22. Everybody was having a Good Time 77

23. A Long Night.. 79

24. Newcomers Move South 82

25. Autumn.. 85

26. Winter in the garden 87

27. Brazil to the rescue 90

28. Mother Squirrel Reaching Home 95

29. Brazil Meets Mother Rat 97

30. Hazel Wakes... 100

31. Mother Squirrel Heals 104

32. Spud... 108

33. Later that Day 110

34. The Swamp 112

35. Leek Goes for Help 117

36. Minding their own business 121

37. The Battle 123

38. The Trail of Father Squirrel................................... 126

39. The Verdict 130

40. The White Blanket.. 135

41. Spring... 140

42. Monty 142

43. The Lake of Truth................................144

44. The Fall of Monty................................148

45. Ed to the Rescue 150

46. In the Potting shed 153

47. Later that day 155

48. That Evening.....................................158

49. Freeing Monty 162

50. The Next Morning..............................165

51. Summer Unfolds................................167

52. Father Squirrel visits Manor Farm 169

53. Mother Squirrel Waits 174

54. Father Squirrel Saved.........................176

55. Out of the mist 179

56. Monty's appearance 183

57. We Come in Peace.............................188

58. The Evening Meeting 191

59. The Day of the Harvest Party 193

60. The Party 195

Acknowledgments

Growing up an undiagnosed Dyslexic shattered my confidence when it came to creating and putting my work out there, so I have a huge thank you to those who first read this book, Jackie, Ruth, Yo and Lisa. Your enthusiasm and encouragement spurred me on to follow through to publication.

Finally, to the beautiful Gardens at Wrest Park, Bedfordshire and those who lovingly tend to them. It's a magical place and I have many happy memories of days spent there with my children.

The Creatures of the Great Garden

The Creatures of the Great Garden

A Map of Wrest Park

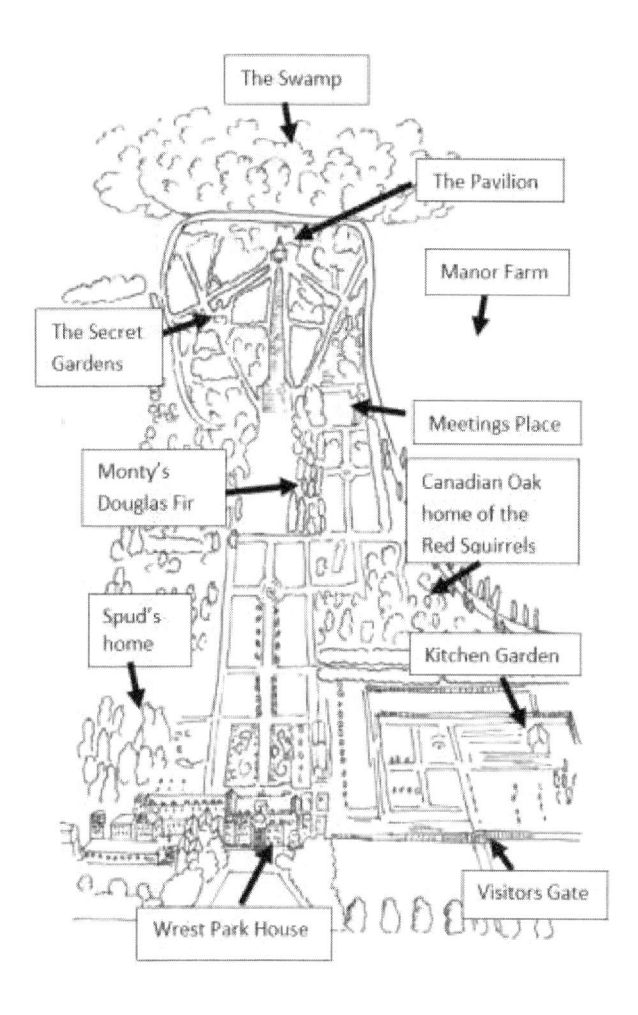

Prologue

Closing Time

Click. A giant, rusty key turned in the last lock as Monty the old Raven swooped in and landed on the large wooden gates at the visitor's entrance of Wrest Park.

"Come to say good night?" Ed, the head gardener, called up to him.

Monty lifted his black beak and fixed his gaze across the garden in attempts to pretend Ed didn't exist. He didn't like or trust humans; he only made a nightly appearance to ensure this one did his job right.

"Be like that," Ed said as he walked to his dusty old car. "Have it your way… but one day, I hope we can be friends."

With that, he disappeared in a cloud of dust down the long, tree-lined drive. Monty waited until Ed's car disappeared out of sight before taking flight to begin his nightly rounds of the Great Garden. He had to be sure no humans had accidentally been locked in. After gliding past the greenhouses and potting sheds in the Kitchen Garden, he swooped over the terraces of the Great House and the beautiful, manicured lawns complete with pretty flowerbeds of vibrant red and deep purple flowers. Continually scanning, Monty soared high into the air and came to rest on top of the giant Blue Douglas Pine in the middle of the garden he called home.

From there, he had the best vantage point over the entire garden. Savoring every inch of it, he sighed and said out loud, "Thank you, Mother Nature. I am so lucky to live in such a beautiful place. It is a garden like no other, and I intend to keep it this way."

After a quick break, Monty continued his rounds, enjoying the cool breeze through his jet-black feathers. Days like this made him feel young again. The only downside of the pleasant weather was that lots of humans came to visit the gardens and picnic in the shade of its beautiful trees.

Monty noticed that despite the hard work of the gardeners, everything that was once green was now scorched brown from the long, hot summer. Scanning from left to right he flew through the tree-lined corridors of the formal woodland gardens. Landing on the huge white dome of the pavilion at the most southerly part of the garden, he looked down at the long lake which led back up to the big house. He waited a few minutes, and when he was fully satisfied, he sent out a piercing squawk which echoed through the gardens and surrounding fields. His cry signaled to the other creatures it was now safe to come out.

CHAPTER 1

Freedom

Monty watched the garden come to life as the residents of the Great Garden appeared from their hiding places, free at last to do as they pleased.

"Look at me," young red squirrels shouted with delight to their parents as they darted up and down trees, testing their climbing skills.

"Keep together, my lovelies," Mother Goose said as she marched across the central lawn, followed by a perfect line of tiny, bright yellow balls of fluff.

Father Fox leisurely licked his lips as he watched them pass by and purred, "Lovely."

"Don't you dare," Mother Fox snarled at him before turning back to watch their two cubs entangled in a play fight.

Spotting the rabbits tumbling across the lawn, Father Fox began to salivate as he muttered under his breath, "Well, maybe a little rabbit then…"

The Long Water, a long rectangular lake at the foot of the Pavilion, was just as busy. The older Badgers and Hedgehogs had woken early to avoid missing anything at the evening meeting, but now, they were searching for a breakfast of bugs at the water's edge.

Monty's attention was drawn to Mother Otter who was bobbing on her back, cradling her baby.

"Be careful," she cried out to the young Ducks practicing their water landings. "Mind where you're going!" she shouted as one narrowly missed her. Then a young Mallard gasped and cried, "Sorry!" when he realised, he'd misjudged his landing distance and was about to collide with a lily pad covered in young Frogs. Crash! The Frogs flew through the air, their limbs outstretched before gracefully disappearing into the glistening blue water. Mother Otter held her breath and anxiously stared in horror until eventually, one by one, each Frog resurfaced, laughing excitedly from the thrill of it.

"Wow! Did you see how high we went?" Rubin, the youngest Frog, croaked with delight.

"What about me!" Russell, the smallest Frog, surfaced and spluttered in amazement, "I must have touched the clouds."

"If you touched the clouds, I must have reached the moon," Richard, who is the clown of the bunch, said as he grinned and bobbed to the surface.

Turning, they all looked over to see Horus the Heron further up the lake practicing his dancing and burst out laughing. Horus's long, grey, gangly legs worked in opposition to the graceful flapping of his wings. He tried to finish his routine with a pirouette, but his feet got stuck in the mud, and he plummeted into the water.

CHAPTER 2

The Evening Meeting

Every evening at sunset, the creatures gather beside the Bowling Green for their evening meeting. Monty took a deep breath and filled his chest with pride as he watched swarms of Dragonflies and Butterflies casually float through the air to come and rest on the grassy banks beside the Frogs. A family of Red Squirrels was surrounded by every species of bird, from the tiniest Wrens and Sparrows to the towering grey mass that was Horus the Heron. The bank was alive with all the colours of the rainbow, from the midnight blue and bright orange of the Kingfishers to the gleaming white Geese and the deep red of the Foxes. He marveled at the scene. The Fox family was surrounded by Ducks, Rabbits, Moles, and Badgers, and they were all relaxing and basking in the last of the evening sun.

Monty scanned the creatures for potential trouble. His battered body, dented beak, and missing tail feathers were testimony to the tough life he'd once lived before finding the Garden. For the first time in Monty's life, he had found peace here, and he intended to keep it that way.

Seeing Narsus the resident male Peacock arrive; Monty rolled his eyes to heaven. Narsus sauntered through the crowd with his magnificent shimmering tail feathers fully displayed for all to see. The rays of the evening sun lit up the dozens of iridescent eyes patterned in his beautiful feathers as he glided up and down the highest point of the amphitheater for maximum effect.

Being used to his behavior, most other creatures ignored him, but a cheeky young Rabbit named Spud shouted, "Give it a rest, Narsus. Nobody cares what you look like."

Irritated, Narsus swiftly changed direction by swishing his huge tail around, sending the young Rabbit tumbling down the grassy bank and causing everybody to laugh.

Monty shook his head. Spud and her brother came to live with Grandfather Rabbit after their mother disappeared. She was young, foolish, and had no sense of danger. In Monty's experience, this would only lead to trouble.

"Come now!" Monty squawked to gain their attention. "There's a lot to get through this evening, and we need to make a start. First, we must discuss our harvest celebration. As you know, the gathering of winter food supplies has gone well, and soon of our feathered friends will be itching to migrate to warmer climates, so it's time to celebrate and give thanks to Mother Nature for all her gifts."

The younger creatures giggled and chattered with excitement. They were really looking forward to the party. They had never been allowed to stay up until sunrise.

"Please! Can I have your attention," Monty continued, "we have a lot to get through." Then, he started allocating jobs. "Mother Mouse, I'm putting you in charge of gathering the blackberries."

"Lovely," she squeaked excitedly, "I know where the best ones are."

Then, he called to Mother Squirrel who by nature was an excitable creature. "Are you ok to collect the nuts?" Just the mention of her name sent her darting up and down with nervous energy.

"Oh! Yes! Yes! Yes!" she chattered excitedly in her high-pitched voice.

Then, he turned to Mother Badger. "If you could please supply some tasty roots."

"Oh, great roots, again," she grumbled. Monty ignored her complaining, knowing it was just her way.

"Right, I think that's the food sorted. Has anybody else got anything to offer?"

The Bees swarmed forward through the crowd. "We've had a productive year. We would be happy to supply some honey."

A rumble of excitement rippled through the crowd. The creatures licked their lips, excited at the thought of this very sweet and rare treat.

Monty nodded his approval and continued, "Right, now onto the entertainment. Mother Goose, can you please organise your choir? Your performance last year on the lake at sunset was spectacular." Mother Goose puffed up her chest feathers with pride.

"And Dragonflies," he continued, "it would be appreciated if you could do your formation fly-by at the same time." The multi-coloured Dragonflies flapped their wings in excitement.

"I'm up for a dance," Horus the Heron interrupted excitedly. "I've been practicing really hard."

"And don't forget us," the young Frogs croaked. "We've nearly perfected our acrobatics." Then, they treated everybody to a mini display as they leapt forward, tumbling through the air, jumping, and leaping until finally, they finished stacked up like a big tower, one on top of the other. Everybody cheered with delight.

"Yes, yes!" Monty shouted above them to regain order. "Save it for tomorrow. Now, let's get busy," he instructed, "we only have tonight to prepare."

"And one more thing," Monty said remembering a job he hadn't covered. "I need a couple of sensible volunteers to go to the orchard and collect some overripe apples." Monty wasn't happy about the animals eating the overripe fruit. It made them all a bit silly, but it had been agreed on this night and this one night only the parents could indulge.

Father Badger and Father Fox shot their paws into the air. "We've got it covered!" they shouted in unison, grinning at each other. Mother Fox glared at Father Fox and said threateningly, "It had better not be like last year when you went missing for two days."

"No dear," Father Fox shouted over his shoulder, "we'll be straight back." Then, they disappeared in the direction of the orchard.

CHAPTER 3

Spud and Radish

Spud the young Rabbit said to her brother Radish, "I wonder what the young Badgers are like?"

Until now, the young Badgers had slept all day and the Rabbits all night, but tomorrow, they would all be out to play together. Radish didn't answer; he continued chewing on a large blade of grass and stared past her as if she didn't exist and Spud's heart broke a little more.

In her misery she was transported back to the day they'd been traveling to the Great Garden to meet their grandpa for the first time. Before they set off, their mother had warned them of the dangers they might encounter along the way. Hopping protectively in front of them, she constantly scanned the long, empty grey road for cars. When she looked forward, Radish would playfully slap Spud on the back of the head, and Spud would try to slap him back before their mother turned to check the road again. Misjudging one of his slaps, Radish sent Spud rolling onto her back. Furious Spud leapt into the air, and as she passed over his head, she caught hold of his big ears and held tight, propelling them into a big fur ball tumbling along the grass verge.

Roaring with laughter, they missed their mothers' frantic screams. Landed in a heap, their laughter was replaced by a deafening roar as they were engulfed in a cloud of dust. Pain instantly filled their bodies, and when the dust settled their mother was gone.

Monty had found them injured and alone at the side of the road got them to their grandpa's burrow in the Great Garden, where they had lived ever since.

Returning her thoughts to the present moment, Spud's paws settled on a permanent fold in her left ear. It was the only visible sign of her injuries. Looking at her brother she wished she could fix him; he hadn't spoken a word since that day. A tear rolled down Spud's cheek as she watched her brother stare into the distance while rhythmically nibbling on another blade of grass. Spud believed if she could cheer him up, make him really happy, then he would be ok again. All her hopes rested on the party tomorrow night. She thought seeing everybody else having fun would remind him what it was like and come back to her. She was determined to make it the best party ever, no matter what it took.

Spud snapped out of her thoughts when she saw her best friend Leek bouncing towards them with her mouth full of fragrant lavender. Placing it in front of Radish, she kindly said, "Thought you might like this."

"Sissy," Spud mocked her friend, but secretly, she was delighted with her efforts to cheer up her little brother.

CHAPTER 4

The visit to the Kitchen Garden

Leek and Spud were unlikely friends. Leek's mother felt sorry for Spud when she first came to live in the garden and made Leek promise to look after her. The two were complete opposites though. Leek was a stickler for the rules, and for Spud, rules only existed to be broken. Seeing Leek gave Spud an idea.

The animals had a pact not to go into the Kitchen Gardens. They figured if they didn't annoy the humans, the humans wouldn't bother them. So far, it had worked. But for Spud, it was a rule she just couldn't live by. The taste of the sweet vegetables tempted her, but it was the thrill of the chase that kept her going back. Her heart racing in her chest made her feel alive, and she loved it. This thrill filled the gaping hole in her chest she felt when she looked at her brother and missed her mum. She also thrived on outsmarting humans. With each visit, there was a different obstacle to overcome. Spud thought the more the gardeners tried to protect something the sweeter it must taste.

"We need to get something special for the party," Spud announced confidently to Leek as they huddled together so nobody could hear them.

"I don't like the sound of this," Leek replied nervously.

"Don't worry. I have a plan," Spud said, smiling.

"That's what worries me," Leek said, quaking.

And before Leek had a chance to talk Spud out of it, she was bounding across the garden in the direction of the Kitchen Garden with a reluctant Leek behind her.

Standing at the foot of the towering red brick wall that surrounded the Kitchen Garden, Spud checked that nobody had followed them before explaining more to Leek.

"I found a drainage hole I can squeeze through," she said as she pulled back some wild daisies that had seeded themselves in it. "I've checked. It runs the whole way through and brings me out at the green houses."

"But what if…" Leek tried to reason.

"No what if's," Spud said firmly. "I have been watching the site for a few days, and the only possible obstacle is Lily."

"Lilly!" Leek wailed in terror.

Lily was the resident Cat who'd been dumped as a Kitten at the gates. Ed had taken pity on her and allowed her to make the garden her home. She was so grateful to him that she had vowed never to let the thieving creatures of the garden ruin his hard work.

Spud said reassuringly, "It has been a hot day, and Lily is somewhere sleeping in the evening sun."

"Yes, but what if she's not?" Leek said assertively.

"That's where you come in," she said, leading her friend to a young sapling beside the huge wall. "Help me strip its bark."

Leek looked at the small tree confused.

"Come on! If Lily chases me, I'll need you to tumble this tree." Spud could see Leek filling her lungs in preparation to list off a hundred reasons why this was a bad idea, but she cut her off. "I know you want to see Radish happy too. Trust me. I have a plan."

Wasting no more time, the two young rabbits stripped back the bark from the young tree. Then, Spud said, "You keep going. Chew away at it until it is just about to fall." Then, she ran in the direction of the drainage hole while shouting over her shoulder, "When I give you the signal, send it crashing to the ground."

Leek continued gnawing and chomping at the soft flesh of the tree, determined not to let her friend down.

Out of the darkness, Spud entered the walled garden. Once inside, she silently tip-toed to the huge glass house. Her heart drummed in her chest, and she felt alive. On previous visits, she'd gone for the easy wins: a head of broccoli, sweet mint, pea pods, anything else she thought Radish might like. She'd often passed the glass houses and wondered what was in there, but the huge windows were usually misted up, so she never got to see inside. However, on her last trip just as she was leaving, she'd spotted a broken pane of glass and ventured over for a peek. What she saw nearly blew her mind. Plants grew everywhere—up the walls, across the floor, hung from the ceiling. Each plant was laden down with multi-coloured fruits, vegetables, and flowers in a huge variety of shapes and sizes. Ever since that glimpse, she had dreamt of this place, and she knew exactly what she wanted and where to find it.

Relieved to see the window hadn't been fixed, Spud carefully climbed through the gap. Her mouth watered as she passed by loaded down branches of cucumbers and shiny red, green, and yellow peppers. There were even some vegetables she'd never seen before. As she passed through, she couldn't help but have a little nibble. First, it

First it was a few strawberries hanging over the narrow path. Then, a nibble of some young lettuce, just the outer leaves she thought. Really enjoying the sweet, fiery taste though, she couldn't stop until her teeth marks were on every leaf. Tearing herself away, she entered a section full of flowers. She thought of her little brother Radish; he would be in heaven here.

CHAPTER 5

Manor farm

That same evening on the other side of the river surrounding Wrest Park lay another world. As the Hedgehog family lay tightly curled up in a ball, sleeping on the floor of their home deep beneath the wheat field. Mother Hedgehog woke early, she questioned had felt a rumble in the earth or if she had imagined it. Holding her breath with fear, she lay motionless as she felt it grow stronger. Snapping into action, she screamed at a sleeping Father Hedgehog, "It's time! It's coming!" Looking franticly around their home to see what she could bring she shouted at him, "Go ahead and find us a safe new home! But remember nowhere near the oak tree and the greedy old Owl!" Then, she looked at her babies and shuddered.

Father Hedgehog leapt into action and darted out of their home as she bellowed after him, "And not by the river that dirty tom cat prowls there!"

Mother Hedgehog was exhausted by the relentless fight for survival, but she had to keep going for her family. They were constantly moving homes to avoid threat after threat—if it wasn't somebody trying to eat them, then it was the humans cutting down their homes or poisoning their food.

Father Hedgehog cautiously peered out of their home and stood in the shadows. Panic rang out beneath the field of golden ripe wheat. Stepping out, he was sent into a spin by a family of Rabbits hurtling past him. One of the Rabbits leapt into the air desperately seeking the safest route out of the field.

"What can you see?" Father Hedgehog cried to the Rabbit, but in a blind panic, the Rabbit continued charging forward, sending the Father Hedgehog flying into the air.

Overhead, Father Hedgehog heard another voice. "Head for the farmhouse, it's safe there." Delighted with the help, he ran out into the light. Just as he began to question who was helping him, a Hawk swooped down and carried him up and away in his sharp talons.

Below ground, Mother Hedgehog continued to snap orders at her children, oblivious to Father Hedgehog's fate.

"But why do we have to move?" Maisie questioned. She didn't understand.

"Stop, child, with all the questions. The humans are coming!" Mother Hedgehog said fearfully. "They are coming with a huge monster like you've never seen before that will eat everything in its way and spit it out as dust. Soon everything in this field will be gone."

CHAPTER 6

In the Kitchen Garden

Despite the distractions of the amazing food, Spud knew exactly what she wanted for the feast, she was in search of tomatoes. She hoped they would remind Radish of their old home and the time they broke into an allotment and stole some for their tea.

Reaching a ladened vine of perfect ripe tomatoes, she spotted a plant with teeny, tiny red peppers hanging from it. Decided as they were so very small, they must be the sweetest peppers ever she would have to have a taste. Greedily, she took a big bite out of one and smugly thought she was right—they were sweet. The sweetness soon changed as a fire started to build inside her. First, her lips tingled, then her throat before an enormous explosion of heat engulfed her mouth. Her eyes watered and sweat ran through her fur and she feared her head would melt. Desperate she scanned the greenhouse for water, she danced to distract herself from the pain. Bouncing around, she accidentally bumped into a stack of empty flowerpots sending them crashing to the floor. The sound echoed through the giant greenhouse. Despite her pain, she momentarily froze. She stood in terror and looked around for any sign of Lily.

Taking a deep breath to calm her nerves and cool her mouth, Spud dashed over to the ripest truss of bright red tomatoes and bit through its stalk releasing it to the floor and she dragged it out of the greenhouse. Finally, as she backed up towards the drainage hole and safety, she relaxed a little and thought of Radish's face when he seen them, when suddenly out of nowhere, Lily pounced blocking her escape route.

"Ha!" Lilly spat into Spud's face. "Thought you'd help yourself to Ed's tomatoes, did you?" Spud froze to the spot, her heart pounded in her head and her stomach churned from the warm stench of Lily's breath on her whiskers.

Lily had waited a long time for this moment, and she intended to savor it. Circling Spud, purring with delight she thought how proud Ed would be of her, he was sure to reward her for this catch. She toyed with Spud, daring her to make a run for freedom. But Spud knew it was futile, she could never outrun Lily. She was trapped and terrified and thought she was going to be sick or pass out. She thought of Radish, how would he manage without her? Spud closed her eyes and braced herself for Lily's next move just as a huge black shadow descended over them. She shivered as wind ran down through her fur and her ears rang with a deafening squawk. Slowly daring to open one eye spud witness Monty's giant flapping wings holding him mid-air in the perfect position to lash out with his sharp feet at Lily.

With Lily distracted defending herself, Spud made a break for freedom dragging the heavy vine behind her. As she entered the drainage hole, she signaled to Leek she was on her way. Spotting her, Lily quickly followed despite Monty's continued attack. Lily squeezed herself into the dark confined space continually lashing out her sharp claws striking a tomato sending salty juice squirting into her eyes. Even half blinded she didn't give up inching herself further and further into the tight space.

Hearing Spud's signal, Leek rose on her front feet and sent powerful kicks of her back legs to the young fir tree, sending it crashing to the ground just as Spud and the last tomatoes appeared from the hole.

"Timber!" Leek shouted with delight as the branches fell perfectly blocking the entrance of the drainage hole. Then she jumped back as Lily's face appeared in the opening. A trapped Lilly screamed from the wall, "I'll get you thieving rotten creatures,"

Spud collapsed exhausted on the grass a distance from the wall. Mistaking the tomato juice on Spud's fur for blood, Leek screamed in panic, "oh no your hurt!" Spud lay there panting too exhausted to speak. Then noticing the tomatoes Leek forgot her concern and exclaimed, "Wow! They look delicious."

Catching her breath, Spud jumped up and said, "Quick let's go! That won't hold Lily for long." and the two friends scampered home, carrying their treasures between them.

Taking a short cut home through the woods Spud's heart began to return to its natural rhythm when out of nowhere a furious Monty appeared. He was a gentle soul who hated conflict, and to be put into the position of defending these two when they were somewhere that was forbidden made him senseless. He jumped up and down, stamping his feet whilst vigorously flapping his wings. He couldn't put into words how angry he felt. Dropping their precious load, Leek cowered behind Spud.

Finally finding his voice, Monty roared into Spud's face, "What were you thinking? Was that worth risking your life for?" He pointed at the battered tomato vine. "Look all around you. You will never go hungry." Then, he flew off in search of their families to see what punishment they would face.

CHAPTER 7

The Great Fire

On the other side of the river, the creatures of Manor Farm prepared for their annual evacuation.

Brazil, a young Grey Squirrel, perched high in a tree watched the huge noisy machine chewing up everything in the neighboring field. Its huge whirling jaws slashed and tore the golden wheat whilst spitting out a large plume of black dust.

Brazil was desperate to help the other creatures but was aware of the Hawk floating high in the sky above him. Distracted by the sound of loud music from a passing car, he watched as a human threw something from the window onto the golden tinder-dry grass verge.

Watching in wonderment, Brazil saw a flickering yellow light dance across the ground then change to red and orange as the wind whipped it up. It swirled into the sky as it hopped across the sun-drenched wheat field. Held in a trance by its magic, he wanted to get a closer look as it gracefully danced from one ear of wheat to the next rendering it black.

Then, terrifying screams of human shouted, "Fire! Fire!" which rang out across Manor Farm, and he realised what he was watching.

Hysteria rose as the wind fanned the flames in constantly changing directions, sending dense black clouds up into the air.

Frogs leapt through the air, croaking. "Leg it! Leg it!" Rabbits thumped warnings on the floor to any sleeping creatures. Startled Badgers and Foxes emerged bleary-eyed from their underground homes as small Birds and Insects flew straight into the sky in a desperate search for safety.

Brazil's eyes burned and his vision blurred as he watched Mother Hedgehog running with her two children between rows of unburnt corn. Abruptly stopping, she screamed as the terrifying orange flames spread and blocked her escape route. He watched her change directions then screamed again as that exit lit up. She made another frantic dash only to find more flames raging there too. Feeling escape was impossible, she let out a terrifying wail, causing Brazil to snap into action. Jumping to the nearest tree to get the best view of the burning field Brazil could see her escape wasn't impossible but she would have to be quick.

"Mother Hedgehog!" he screamed. "Keep going! There's a gap. You can make it to the river." But it was useless Mother Hedgehog remained in a huddle on the floor. With no heed for his own safety, Brazil took a huge gulp, filling his lungs with clean air, then dove into the burning field and raced towards Mother Hedgehog and her terrified children.

Ignoring the intensity of the heat, he darted across the burning cornfield with only one thing on his mind—getting Mother Hedgehog and her children safely to the river. With no time to explain, he wrapped his singed tail around her spikey neck and tried to drag her in the direction she needed to go. The harder he pulled, the more she tried to roll up in a defensive spikey ball. Brazil's lungs started to run out of oxygen, and he feared it might be all over.

Then out of nowhere, a mighty squawk came from above.

"Do as he say," Monty boomed down at her.

The sight of a Raven hovering above brought Mother Hedgehog to her senses, and she grabbed Brazil's tail, and he ran forward, dragging the family behind him with Monty's guidance from the air. They ran as fast as they could until suddenly, a glimpse of blue sky could be seen as they briefly took flight before being plunged into the cooling waters of the river.

CHAPTER 8

Screams of Terror

With fearful, heavy hearts, Spud and Leek picked up what remained of the vine and slowly made their way home. As they inched through the long tree line avenue, they could feel the rumble beneath their feet. Sensing this was not good they jumped into a nearby bush to hide. In seconds flocks of Birds darkened the sky and Squirrels flew through the trees over their heads.

It felt like every creature in the Great Garden was on the move. Leaving their tomatoes hidden they followed the stampede. As the trees cleared on the riverbank, they could see a black, ugly cloud growing on the other side of the river, swallowing up the blue summer sky.

The creatures sat on the riverbank in horror and watched the yellow flame turning everything it touched black. They could almost feel the heat of the flames from where they sat. They were powerless to help. Some tried to cover their eyes, but they couldn't block out the sound of desperate cries from the creatures on the other side of the water.

Eventually there were screaming sirens and flashing blue lights as huge red machines appeared. They sat helpless as the humans worked hard late into the evening until finally, the fire was out.

As darkness fell, Monty returned to the garden to find the creatures still huddled on the riverbank in a strange eerie silence.

"Go!" he commanded. "Go home and gather what you can to help our fellow creatures. I will see how best we can assist. We will meet at daybreak to formulate a plan." Then, he took to the air and disappeared out of sight in the smoky night sky.

CHAPTER 9

Dawn the next morning

The next morning, as daylight peered over the Pavilion, hours before the Gardens opened to the humans, every creature was present in the amphitheater waiting to see how they could help the residents of Manor Farm. Taking his usual stance on top of the Bay Tree, Monty called them to order.

"Please!" he shouted. "Let's not waste any time getting down to business. As you all know, our neighbors in Manor Farm had something terrible happen to them yesterday evening. I have been over this morning, and some are missing. Many are hurt.

All with minor injuries, I'm pleased to say, but they need our urgent assistance," he concluded.

A family of Mice dragged bags of grain to the middle of the crowd said. "We are happy to help,"

"Us too!" said the Frogs producing their offering of help which was quickly followed by the Rabbits who came bearing fresh herbs and young nettles.

"This is all very decent of you," Monty said, thanking them all, "and I am sure it will be appreciated, but they will need much more than this. They have lost everything—their homes, winter food supplies. They have nothing. They are in a terrible state as I am sure you can imagine."

There was silence as they all thought of their fellow creatures. "What they have asked," Monty said after taking a long pause, unsure of what the reaction would be. "What they would like is to move in with us for the winter until they have had time to rebuild and sort themselves out."

Carrot, a large Rabbit, broke the silence, "What? All of them?! But there won't be enough food for us all."

"Oh, I'm sure we have enough to go around," a sleepy Hedgehog said.

"It's all right for you," Carrot continued, "you sleep all winter. How will you feel if you wake in the spring, and your food store is empty?"

Father Hedgehog, who was always in a good mood, chuckled his reply, "They will have to find it first. I've hidden it well.

"The more the merrier!" Father Fox said, licking his lips.

"What about the other farms?" Father Squirrel protested. "Why can't they go there?"

"Some have," Monty explained, "but they can't take them all."

Silence fell over the group as they considered everything. Then, Father Squirrel burst forward from the crowd. "If there are Squirrels, they must be Red like us!"

Monty was silent for a moment. He feared this might be a problem as he knew all the squirrels were grey, "I afraid I can't guarantee that,"

Father Squirrel bounced around at lightning speed shrieking, "What do you mean can't guarantee it? We are the only Red Squirrels in the county. You let that dirty lot in, and you can say goodbye to that."

Monty shouted over his protests, and with a heavy heart, he said, "I'm sorry. I need your decision, and soon. Their future is in our hands."

Muttering steadily grew amongst the animals as they began to voice their concerns to each other. Most of them complained about overcrowding and food supplies.

Monty shouted over them, "I said I'd give them your answer tonight when the garden closes. I suggest you all go home and think it through."

Spud couldn't help herself and blurted out, "But what about the Harvest Party?"

The muttering stopped, and all the creatures glared at her. Monty marched over to Spud and blasted furiously into her face, "Do you really expect us to celebrate when our fellow creatures have suffered so much?!" The fire had distracted him from dealing with young Spud and the foolish Leek—something he planned to rectify as soon as things settled down. He vowed to make sure they were punished.

Spud hung her head; the others thought it was in shame, but she was devastated she had lost the chance of seeing her brother smile again.

CHAPTER 10

Later that Day

Visitors to the garden weren't deterred by the nearby fire. In fact, there was more than usual, all curious to see for themselves the path of devastation that had made the evening news.

The extra visitors didn't keep Father Squirrel in hiding. He jumped from tree to tree, trying to work off some of his fury and a sense of pending doom, but it was no good. He spotted Mother Goose with her six fluffy chicks all snuggled around her hiding in the long grass beside the great lake. Dangling dangerously from a thin branch overhead, Father Squirrel yelled to her, "Do you really want those dirty, smelly creatures from Manor Farm coming to live with you?"

Mother Goose looked at him in horror. "Shh!" she snapped. "You'll show the humans where we are hiding."

"The humans will be the least of your worries if that dirty rabble comes to live with us!" he shouted back at her.

Mother Goose gingerly peeped her head over the top of the tall grass to see if any humans were nearby. Seeing none, she screamed back at him, "Go Away! You are upsetting my babies." Then, she turned her attention to her chicks and said, "Don't mind Father Squirrel. He's just being silly."

"Silly! Silly!" he exploded. "You will not be saying silly when that lot move in and turn our garden into a pigsty." Then, he took off, jumping from branch to branch and at times almost skimming the heads of the humans who walked the tree-lined avenues. This caused great excitement among the little ones who screamed with delight at his appearance. He was fearless in his fury, taking chances he would normally never dream of.

Then, he spotted Narsus who was putting on a display for the Humans. They gathered around him as he glided up and down the path fanning his spectacular tail, his head held high as if he didn't even realise, they were there. Father Squirrel darted across the lawn and screamed at him, "The dirty, smelly farm creatures will make us all sick! They will bring diseases; you wait and see!"

"Go away," Narsus hissed as he watched the humans' attention turn to the angry Squirrel. Then, he turned sharply, causing a draft from his massive tail to knock Father Squirrel off his feet. This added to the Squirrel's fury, making him jump back up and screech louder.

"You wait and see! They will make you sick!" he screamed over his shoulder as he headed off in search of somebody that would listen to his fears.

Finding himself at the entrance of the Fox's home, Father Squirrel cupped his mouth with his tiny paws and yelled into the long, dark tunnel burrowed under a giant cedar tree.

"Father Fox! Are you awake?" He didn't feel quite so brave when Father Fox emerged from the darkness, his eyes squinting in the bright sunlight. He took his time yawning and stretching, then he moved close to Father Squirrel's face. Father Squirrel could feel the warmth of Father Fox's breath as it moved through his fur, sending a shiver down his back. Father Fox moved even closer then yawned again, nearly sucking Father Squirrel into his huge gaping mouth. "I am now," he snapped. "This had better be important."

"We, we, we… have to stop, stop the Manor Farm creatures from moving into our Great Garden," Father Squirrel stammered, his eyes wide with terror.

Father Fox yawned again as he said, "Why do we need to do that?"

"Because they will eat other creatures, and you will get the blame and be thrown out of the garden and have to live in the swamp with the Rats and Minx!"

"What's to say I won't eat a few tasty creatures and blame them instead?" he said, licking his lips and flicking droplets of saliva all over Father Squirrel. Then, he moved even closer to Father Squirrel and purred, "Does anybody know you're here?" He licked his lips again.

Father Squirrel leapt backwards and flew up the nearest tree and out of Father Fox's reach. As he flew through the trees, Father Fox's roars of laughter igniting Father Squirrels fury again.

Blast them all, he thought, why can't they see a disaster was about to happen? Then, he spotted Carrot the fat Rabbit who couldn't go a whole day in hiding without coming out to eat. Carrot was happily chomping his way through a wild geranium that was growing in one of the secret garden rooms. "Make the most of that," Father Squirrel shouted at him. "When the Farm creatures come, there will be none left."

Startled, Carrot darted around in panic before eventually locating the direction of the voice. He looked up to see Father Squirrel hanging high above him.

"What are you trying to do?" he panted, recovering from the shock.

"Warn you! Get you to realise what a terrible mistake it would be to let those greedy creatures into our garden!" Father Squirrel shouted.

Carrot scanned the area, terrified a human would appear or worse—one of their nasty dogs. "Keep your voice down," he said, "I get where you're coming from, but what can I do about it?"

"We need to stick together," Father Squirrel answered. "We have to stop them!" Nodding his head in agreement, Carrot shot off as Father Squirrel watched his white tail bobbing into the distance and shouted, "tell everyone you meet! We must stop them!"

Feeling he had finally found an ally, Father Squirrel felt inspired to continue his mission to keep those dirty, filthy creatures out of his Great Garden.

CHAPTER 11

Evening Meeting

As the creatures gathered for the evening meeting, Monty could sense the tension in the air. He knew he would have to handle this very carefully. He had become aware of Father Squirrel's strange behavior that day and sensed trouble.

"Right," Monty said taking charge, "I thought we should have a short discussion before we vote on whether the Manor Farm creatures can come and winter with us. Who would like to go first?" He gestured his wing to the center of the amphitheater.

Seizing his chance, Father Squirrel sprang forward and said with authority, "The creatures of Manor Farm are lazy! If they looked after their own homes, they wouldn't need ours. They are dirty! You can smell them from here." He danced around, addressing each creature with their worst fears. "I'm telling you, Father Hedgehog you will wake one winter's day to find your winter store empty, and you and your family will starve. Mother Goose—will your babies be safe with Manor Foxes running around over here? They will not be able to follow our basic rule of not eating your babies."

Mother Goose clutched her young tightly under her wing and shivered at the thought.

Finally, he turned his attention to the Rabbits. "They will steal and trash our beautiful home, and it will never be the same again," he concluded. He felt satisfied he had made his case.

"He made a powerful argument," Carrot shouted, backing Father Squirrel. He signaled to the other Rabbits who thumped their back legs in support and were quickly followed by the Mice. Then, the Hedgehogs began cheering, and the Ducks and Geese started clucking. Before long, the entire crowd was cheering, and Father squirrel relaxed. Finally, they are listening, he thought, everything is going to be ok.

Monty waited for the cheers to subside before he flew down into the center of the circle of creatures and quietly spoke. "Mother and Father Hedgehog, do you remember when I found you three years ago homeless and terrified on the side of the road? I invited you in, and you have been here ever since." The Hedgehogs hung their heads and blushed.

Then he turned to Grandpa Rabbit, "When your daughter was killed, how did you feel when I brought your grandchildren Spud and Radish here to live with us?" Grandpa Rabbits' eyes filled with tears thinking of his beautiful girl.

Then, Monty spoke to the Otters, "When your lake at Mill Farm dried up in the hot summer five years ago, were you not welcomed here?" Then, he hopped over to the Geese and said, "Remember your great grandparents were welcomed here when they got sick on their long migration flight, and you have been welcome ever since."

Silence fell over the Great Garden as they absorbed what he was saying. They had forgotten how tough their lives had been before they had come to the Great Garden and how much they all had to be grateful for living in this beautiful place. They had forgotten the worlds they had escaped, surrounded by hardship, fear, and hunger. In the Great Garden, they had abundant food and support from each other in times of need. It wasn't just a beautiful place; it was an idyllic safe and peaceful home in which to raise their families.

Pausing, Monty gave them time to process his words. Remembering the urgency of the situation, he said with authority, "Ok, time to vote. Those who want the residents of Manor Farm to winter with us, stand to my right." He flapped open his right wing so there was no confusion. "Those who don't, stand to my left."

Slowly, the creatures shuffled around, and despite Father Squirrels' animated protests, they cast their votes until finally, it was clear. Every creature except the Squirrel family stood on Monty's right.

"Well, let's get on with it!" Monty commanded as he rose into the air. "I'll go and tell them the good news."

CHAPTER 12

The Evacuation

The creatures quickly made their way to the river's edge to see how they could help, but they weren't prepared for what awaited them.

A flock of soring Birds of prey hovered in the sky in search of another easy meal. Families of small creatures clung to anything that would float and sheltered under the tall reads on the riverbank. Terrified families of Moles clung cold and wet to bobbing apples, Mice lay on leaves, and young Rabbits held on to branches. Even bits of rubbish the humans had discarded, like crisp packets and plastic bottles, became lifesaving rafts for the small creatures. Behind them on the charred riverbank lay rows of exhausted, unrecognisable blackened creatures hoping for a miracle.

The sight of Monty lifted their spirits. "I come with good news," he delighted in telling them. "Let the evacuation begin!" And with no time to waste, he was joined by the Creatures of the Great Garden, and he started issuing instructions.

"Frogs, could you float injured Insects across on lily pads? Otters, take the Toads on your stomachs. Geese and Ducks—can you gently cradle the injured Squirrels on your soft backs? And Foxes, carefully load the baby Ducks into your open mouths and safely deposit them on the other side of the river?"

Pleased with the plan, the creatures of the Great Garden eagerly swam across the river to help. Despite desperation and exhaustion, the Mother Ducks screeched, "No way am I letting Foxes anywhere near my babies!" Another Duck said in way of explanation, "We've heard life is different in your garden, but to us, a Fox is a Fox."

"Ok," Monty conceded his plan would not work. Taking their lead, he asked, what would make them more comfortable?

"Toads are you happy to go with the Otters?" they croaked. "Yep." Then, to the Mice, "Are you ok to travel with the Ducks and Frogs?" There was a weak squeak of agreement. Then, he turned to the injured Insects. "Are you happy to travel across the river on the Fox's heads?" They fluttered their agreement.

When every creature was happy, Monty said, "Right! Be quick!" He looked up into the sky at the hovering Hawks and red Kites. "You lot get moving whilst myself and Horus distract that lot."

"Wait!" Mother Hedgehog pleaded as she and her children delicately balanced on a floating log. "What about Father Hedgehog? We can't go without him."

Monty replied gently, "Let's get you to safety, and I promise I will come back and look for him." Then, he gave a signal to start and took to the air with Horus.

Circling above to protect the operation, Monty realised this may not be as simple as he thought. These creatures experienced a different world than those from the Great Garden, and it may take some time for them all to understand each other.

As each creature reached dry land the newcomers were checked out at Mother Squirrels recovery center. They were assessed for injuries, but it was mostly just singed feet, fur, and feathers but for Mother Hedgehog, it was a broken heart. She continually asked everyone she met, "Have you seen Father Hedgehog?" Each time, the answer was negative.

When all the newcomers were fed and settled for the night, Monty took stock of the last 24 hours. He was so proud of the way the creatures of the Great

Garden welcomed the newcomers. The Geese spruced up their old nests. The Mice shared their winter store with other Mice. Even the Badger family opened their home and welcomed a family of Rabbits.

Monty was exhausted. "I'm getting too old for all this drama," he said to himself. It had been a long day, and there was still lots to do, but it would have to wait until tomorrow. Returning home to his lonely nest, Monty curled up and instantly fell into a deep sleep.

CHAPTER 13

Father Squirrel

Everybody slept well that night except Father Squirrel. He was livid. He couldn't contain his anger. "Traitor!" He screamed at her when she came home that evening. He was furious with her for helping the newcomers.

"I hope you're happy. This will be the end of us Red Squirrels," he screamed.

"I didn't help any Grey Squirrels," she said, defending her actions.

"No, but they are all as bad as each other, just wait and see. They will destroy everything!" he screamed in fury as he disappeared into the darkness.

He sprinted up and down every tree trying to exhaust his fury. He couldn't understand why nobody would listen to him. Why couldn't they all see this was a disaster?

CHAPTER 14

Brazil's New Home

Brazil and his mother searched for a new home in the most southerly part of the garden. They ignored the blood-chilling scream from the swamp that regularly echoed across the damp, marshy land. It had been agreed for peace's sake the Grey Squirrels would stay as far away from the Red Squirrels as possible.

Searching high in an ash tree, his mother shouted, "Over here! I think I've found our new home." Following his mother's voice and climbing high into the maple tree, he saw her sitting proudly in an abandoned Bird's nest.

"It's comfortable," she said happily. "There are even a few feathers from its last occupant to keep us warm this winter." She smiled.

"You're always looking for the positive," Brazil said as he smiled back at her.

"And look at the views," she said waving her arm. "Now why don't you go out and explore?"

"I have no one to explore with," Brazil said sadly.

"I know my love," she said, sympathetically. "But I told you, there was no room in the other fields for us, so we had to come here. It's going to be a long winter if you just sit here. Why don't you go and help your father collect nuts for our winter store and let me get on with fixing this place up?" Dutifully, Brazil headed out in search of his father.

CHAPTER 15

The Next Morning

Mother Squirrel woke with a feeling of dread in her stomach. Something was wrong, but she didn't know what. Looking around, she realised Father Squirrel was missing and her mind raced. He hadn't come home last night. What if he was trapped and hurt somewhere? What if he had fallen in the river and the weight of his big wet tail stopped him from getting out? She whimpered as a film played in her head of all the bad things that might have happened to him.

Glancing at her sleeping children, she decided to go look for him. As she flew through the canopy, skillfully jumping from tree to tree, she noticed a path of devastation unfolding beneath her.

"Hey!" Father Hedgehog shouted up to her furiously. "Did you see who smashed open my winter store?"

"Sorry, no, I have no idea," Mother Squirrel shouted back surveying all his winter food scattered across the ground. Moving on, she saw the Mice family huddled together crying as they stared at their berries all mashed to a pulp. Torn, she wanted to stop and help, but her need to find Father Squirrel was greater.

As the creatures woke cries rang out across the garden as more and more creatures discovered their winter food supplies had been destroyed. Reaching the edge of the lake, Mother Squirrel yelped at the sight of all the Harvest Party food either tramped onto the ground or floating in the lake. Beneath her, more and more creatures gathered to survey the damage.

"No!" Spud screamed in horror when she saw her precious vine with only one remaining tomato.

Standing in the middle of the devastation, Monty noticed a large portion of the over-ripe apples were missing and glared over at Father Badger and Father Fox.

"Well!" Monty said, flying up beside them. "Can you account for yourselves last night?"

"What?" they said together in shock. "Why are you asking us? It wasn't us!"

"Can you blame me for asking?" Monty asked. "Especially after last year's incident when you gorged yourselves on the overripe apples and got into a fight."

"It had better not be you," Mother Fox snarled at Father Fox. They were on their last warning in the garden after the disappearance of the other male Peacock last year. Monty was sure Father Fox had eaten him, but he just could not prove it. They knew one more strike and they would be banished to the marsh.

"It wasn't me love," Father Fox pleaded with her, "I was with you all night."

Instantly she changed from accuser to defender. "That's right! He was with me helping to settle our guests," she said with relief and delight.

Mother Badger chipped in, "You can ask our new guests. Father Badger was home all night too." Both animals looked to their wives with gratitude.

"Then, who would do such a terrible thing?" Monty asked, surveying all the damage.

CHAPTER 16

Mother Squirrels

Fearing the worst, Mother Squirrel scurried up the tallest trees hoping to see Father Squirrel. It was coming close to opening time for the garden, and soon, there would be loads of humans. She didn't like to be too far away from her children when they were around.

A shiver ran down her spine when she heard Monty's squawk warning that the gardens were open to humans. Her instincts were to dart for the safety of home, but she didn't want to give up on Father Squirrel just yet. She knew deep down he was good and kind, but for some reason, a kind of madness had overtaken him.

Hearing the familiar sound of snoring, she darted across the great lawn to a pile of leaves and found a bunch of half-eaten rotten apples and Father Squirrel. Her heart broke, and she cried seeing him in that state. Then, her sadness was replaced with terror as she saw the humans walking towards them.

Desperately, she shook him by the shoulders and tried to wake him, but it was no use. He wouldn't wake. She wanted to shout at him but didn't dare for fear of drawing attention to them. So, she tried to drag him by the tail across the grass to safety. She pulled and pulled with all her might, but the distance to the edge of the lawn didn't get any smaller.

Then she heard the small human's voice shout excitedly, "Oh look Mummy! Squirrels! If I catch one, can I take it home?" The bigger humans laughed, and the little human dashed excitedly towards her. Mother Squirrel froze in terror as the little human got closer and closer and bigger and bigger.

Snapped out of her trance by a voice she didn't recognise, "Hay! Hay! Do ya want help?" Looking behind her, Mother Squirrel saw a big fat Rat hauling herself out of the river. Looking in disbelief Mother

Squirrel said, "You shouldn't be in the Great Garden."

"Do ya want help, or a debate on where I should or shouldn't be?" replied the Rat lazily.

Mother Squirrel turned back to look at the little human still charging towards her. "Help! Please, help, help!" Mother Squirrel squealed.

The enormous Rat simply waddled over in front of the Squirrels and stood there smiling. The adult humans spotted the Rat, and their relaxed manner instantly turned to panic. They dropped their picnic and dashed after the little human, screaming, "No! Come back, come back!" The Rat chuckled to herself and watched the humans scoop up the little one and hurriedly head off in a different direction. Studying Father Squirrels fruit-stained body the rat said to Mother Squirrel, "Do ya want a hand getting him to the river? I'm guessing you need him cleaned up."

Open-mouthed and unable to believe she was asking a Rat for help, Mother Squirrel nodded. The Rat leisurely dragged Father Squirrel to the river's edge, then she put one foot to Father Squirrel's back and sent him tumbling down the riverbank. Finally, there was a big splash as he contacted the cold water. The Rat squealed with delight as he bobbed up and down, spluttering and gasping for air. He was shocked and confused and tried to scream, but instead he kept taking in big gulps of water. The Rat roared laughing then joined him in the water and pushed him safely onto the riverbank with Mother Squirrel fussing over him. As she disappeared back into the water, she shouted over her shoulder to Mother Squirrel, "Don't forget, you owe me!"

Father Squirrel lay on the riverbank gradually gaining his whereabouts as Mother Squirrel darted around hysterically, screeching, "Oh no, no, no we are in so much trouble! You ate the rotten apples; we'll be kicked out of the garden!" she wailed.

"Shut up, I need to think," he said rubbing his sore head. Startled, Mother Squirrel gulped down a sob and ran in the direction of home, calling back, "It's late, we need to get back to the children!"

CHAPTER 17

Emergency meeting

Monty puzzled over the events of the night before. He questioned: Who could have done so much damage in one night? He cursed himself for sleeping so soundly, but after all the drama in Manor Farm, he'd been exhausted. Peering out of his nest, he noted the beautiful summer's day had dramatically given way to the first autumn storm. The sunny morning was a distant memory as he watched the driving rain and gusting winds rage through the garden, making the world feel even more unsettled.

Ed decided to close the gardens to the humans for fear of a loose branch or giant pinecones from the Douglas fir falling and hurting a human. Along with the weather, the mood in the Garden had changed with the realisation that winter was just around the corner. They had extra mouths to feed and no winter supplies. Seizing this opportunity, Monty called an emergency meeting later that day to see how they could try to put right all the damage.

The meeting was held in one of its secret garden rooms. It was far enough away from the potting sheds where the gardeners sheltered from the storm. Swooping in early, he sat on the head of a human statue looking at a book. From there, he scanned the oval-shaped space walled with perfectly manicured Beech hedges with tall Hazel trees peering over the top. When Monty was happy it was safe, he signaled for all to come. Slowly, the creatures arrived with their heads hung low in defeat.

Monty did his usual scan to see if anyone was acting oddly, but all that was clear was the divide. Newcomers sat on one side looking very uncomfortable, and the creatures of the Great Garden sat on the other.

The only creatures to break ranks were the pitiful sight of Mother Hedgehog as she shuffled through the crowd trailed by her two children. "Have you seen Father Hedgehog?" she repeatedly questioned. Monty made a mental note to fly over Manor Farm again to see if he could find any news, but he didn't hold out much hope. His feathers tingle, picking up the tension building in the room so took his position and start the meeting.

"Good news," Monty announced, trying to sound positive and lift their moods. "The weather is on our side. The gardens are closed because of the storm so we can start work to replenish our stores immediately."

"What!" Father Squirrel sprang forward, shouting hysterically. "What we all want to know," then he turned and stared at the Newcomers, "is, who ate all our food?"

"Yes!" Father Mouse squeaked, and the crowd followed.

"Father Squirrel was right," Carrot the fat Rabbit said. "He tried to warn us. They are lazy." He said pointing at the newcomers. "Yes!" voices from the crowd added.

"I'm not feeding them!" an unusually grumpy Father Hedgehog said, still seething, that somebody had found his food store.

"Ye!" They all joined in.

"I'm sorry!" Monty said firmly. "The investigations will have to wait. Our priority now is to get our winter food, and then, I promise you, we will find out who was responsible for the horrendous act." Quickly allocating jobs he dismissed them hoping a hard day's work would tire their fury.

Everybody got stuck in—even Mother Nature helped by blowing nuts and fruit from the trees, making the process much easier. As the evening light faded and darkness enveloped the garden, the clouds parted as if by magic, revealing a full moon to light their way and enable them to continue working late into the night.

Exhaustion didn't tire the creature's chatter; instead, it seemed to feed it. Mother Goose said to Grandpa Rabbit, "I don't know what all the fuss is about. My new guests are really lovely. They don't eat much and are no trouble."

Grandpa Rabbit's hearing wasn't the best, despite his big ears repeated what he thought she'd said to Father Otter, "Mother Goose said her new guests are really muddy, don't eat much, and are real trouble."

Then, Father Otter who still had water in his ears met Mother Fox and told her, "Mother Goose said her new guests are muddy, they eat loads, and are real trouble."

Mother Fox, who was delighted to hear someone other than her family being blamed, told it to anyone who would listen. Even Mother Goose, who assumed they were all talking about a different

Mother Goose, changed her mind about her own house guests.

Soon the creatures of the Great Garden were convinced the newcomers had trashed the garden and wished they'd listened to Father Squirrel.

CHAPTER 18

Mother Squirrel returns home

Mother Squirrel returned home that night with her three children. She was so proud of them for working so hard. They had managed to replace their winter food, but she was exhausted. It had felt like the longest day of her life.

She looked at her family. Her daughter Hazel and sons Cashew and Pecan were growing up fast. She paused at the bottom of the Canadian Oak that was home.

"What's wrong, Mama?" Hazel said, concerned.

Mother Squirrel looked into her daughter's big brown, innocent eyes and could have wept. For the first time in her life, Mother Squirrel didn't want to go home. She feared Father Squirrel was raging around the place in one of his spiteful moods.

Standing in the cool evening air, she heard "Pst!" then "Pst!" again. "Over here! I'm in the Holly Bush." Recognising the voice of the Rat who'd helped her that morning, Mother Squirrel anxiously darted about on the spot and screamed at her children, "Bed now this minute! Off you go, shoo!"

When she was sure they were out of earshot, Mother Squirrel said, "What are you doing here?"

Stepping out of the shadows, the Rat said, "I've come to cash in the favor you owe me."

"Me? Oh me! What me? Oh no, no, no!" Mother Squirrel wailed in a total panic, running in large circles around the Rat. Feeling dizzy, the Rat put out her paw and pinned Mother Squirrel's fluffy tail to the ground, bringing her to a sudden stop. Slowly turning her head, she came nose to nose with the Rat. "We had a deal," the Rat said menacingly into her face. Mother Squirrel gulped and in a tiny voice replied, "I don't remember a deal."

Slowly and even more menacingly, the Rat replied, "Oh I think you do. Should I jog your memory by telling the other perfect creatures about Father Squirrel's partying ways?"

Mother Squirrel's eyes widened in terror.

"Now, you listen, and you listen up well. I need food and I need it now," the Rat said calmly.

"But..." Mother Squirrel squeaked.

"No buts!" the Rat demanded. "Food and now!" The Rat removed her paw from Mother Squirrel's tail and waddled back in the direction of the Holly Bush, saying over her shoulder, "Leave it under here and make it snappy."

Mother Squirrel stood rooted to the spot trying to process what had just happened. Then, the voice from under the bush snapped, making her jump, "I said now!" Mother Squirrel went into a frenzy of dragging nuts and seeds from her winter stash in the direction of the Holly Bush. Eventually, the Rat smiled and said, "That'll do for now, but don't forget my breakfast in the morning." Then, the Rat gathered up the food and waddled off, disappearing into the shadows.

CHAPTER 19

The Divide Grows

As the watery sun crept into the autumn sky the following morning, creatures appeared in the amphitheater for a morning meeting. Monty surveyed the sea of angry, tired faces looking back at him. His heart ached to see them like this. The atmosphere in the garden was toxic, and he knew he had to do something. Calling the meeting to order, he announced, "On reflection, I may have been a bit hasty cancelling our Harvest Party. With our success yesterday replenishing our food stores, I think it may be even more important than ever that we all give thanks to Mother Nature, and I mean all, it is time we welcome our new guests."

"Yes!" Spud screamed with delight and flipped backwards, summersaulting in mid-air and everybody laughed.

"No way!" Father Squirrel shouted and leaped forward. "You can't expect me to sit with that!" He pointed at the newcomers; his face screwed up in disgust.

"Our guests," Monty said firmly, "will be treated with respect!" Regaining control of the meeting, he added, "I think in light of recent events it's a good time to remind us all of the rules of our garden." Flapping his wings, he gestured to the other creatures to join in.

"1. We must always tell the truth, "He led, and the reluctant crowd mumbled.

"2. We must always work hard," the chorus of voices slowly grew.

"3. We must always keep our promises," Mother Squirrel shot a glance at Father Squirrel who quickly looked away.

"4. We must always treat others as we would like to be treated," the volume strengthened. Then, creatures of the Great Garden boomed, looking at the newcomers,

"5. Never steal another creature's food!"

Trying to calm it a little, Monty said, "And most importantly," and the creatures of the Great Garden replied:

"6. Never eat each other!"

"And what happens to anybody who breaks these rules?" Monty said, staring at Father Fox.

"What? Why are you looking at me?" Father Fox said defensively, and Mother Fox stamped on his foot. He yelped and glared at her, then replied quietly, "They're kicked out and have to live with the Rats and Minx in the swamp."

"Sorry, didn't quite catch that?" Spud called out, feeling very jubilant that the party was back on.

Father Fox cleared his throat and howled, "They have to leave the garden and go live in the swamp."

Father Squirrel leapt forward and tried to protest just as Monty cried, "Off with you!" Flapping his big black wings, he knocked Father Squirrel off his feet. "Off, shoo, and get ready for a great night tonight." Father Squirrel scrabbled to his feet in time to see the last creature leave the amphitheater.

CHAPTER 20

The Harvest Party

Monty landed on top of the pavilion and surveyed the magnificent sight below him. On the lawn by the long lake lay a beautiful carpet of autumnal leaves. Carefully placed upon the middle of the center stage were treats for every creature stacked high: nuts, seed, and berries crowned with another oozing honeycomb from the Bees as well the vine with the one remaining tomato.

Flower garlands hung from the trees and around each creature's neck as they all sat around the feast. Newcomers and creatures of the Great Garden alike sat side by side, united in giving thanks to Mother Nature for her bounty.

The Harvest Party was put together in record time, and Monty was happy to see all the creatures finally working as a team. He noted that nobody worked harder than young Spud and Leek, and he hoped they'd learned their lesson. He even reconsidered telling their families about their trip to the Kitchen Garden.

CHAPTER 21

Father Squirrel's Pain

Father Squirrel paced up and down the trunk of the Canadian Oak. The happy sounds of the party drifted up through the trees, and it sickened him. Celebrate—what was there to celebrate? He raged. He was furious with Mother Squirrel for mixing with those creatures and even worse taking their three.

Then, he thought of his beautiful daughter Hazel, her huge brown eyes and perfect red fur and his blood to boil again at the thought of just one of the Grey Squirrels even looking at her. His rage steadily grew until he couldn't take it anymore and went in search of more overripe apples to escape his pain.

CHAPTER 22

Everybody was having a Good Time

When the food was eaten, they sat back to watch the entertainment. First, the migrating Birds gathered in mass in the evening sky, casting a huge shadow over the garden. Then, they separated into smaller groups making magical patterns before changing direction and shooting at top speed across the sky towards each other. The crowd gasped then went wild, cheering and thumping their feet with delight.

The whole time the display was on, Narsus strutted up and down the garden showing off, his long feathers outstretched into a magnificent display. Seizing their chance, the young Swallows shot sideways through the narrow gaps in his tail feathers, sending Narsus into a spin. The crowd roared with laughter as the big show off stumbled and rolled down the grassy bank and landed in a heap, his tail feathers all tangled.

A cheer then went up as Horus started his dancing display, his long, bendy legs knocking together and dull grey, feathered wings showing no sense of timing, but the audience loved it. "Encore! Encore!" They all screamed when finished, and Horus set off again.

As Monty surveyed the crowd, he was quietly pleased to see them all sitting together. The newcomers and the creatures of the Great Garden were happy, sharing food and enjoying the great entertainment. Then, his eye was drawn to poor Mother Hedgehog who was cradling her two children. Despite all the fun and jolliness, they sat in pure misery, heartbroken.

CHAPTER 23

A Long Night

As night turned into day, Monty watched the creatures singing and dancing happily together. Newcomers and residents were having fun, swinging each other around and falling in heaps, laughing so hard as if it were the funniest thing that had ever happened. Their carefree mood fueled by the over-ripe apples sent laughter into the air.

Then, without warning, laughter turned to screams of terror, "Spit him out!" Mother Goose from Manor Farm screamed at Father Fox. "Spit him out!" She viciously pecked at him, sending tiny clouds of his red fur up into the air. Father Fox squealed in pain as each lump of fur was torn from his skin.

"I don't know," he pleaded, then yelped, "Ow! What you're talking about!"

"Spit my boy out!" she hissed. "I saw your mouth full, and now, my only baby is gone!"

The other Manor Farm Geese joined in, plucking lumps out of Father Fox.

"I didn't!" he yelped between bites. Then, he screamed out, "Ouch!" in severe pain, as Mother Fox bit into his leg. "Spit it out," she growled furiously at him.

Shocked, the Geese momentarily stopped, just long enough to hear a little voice behind them, "I'm over here, Mama."

Mother Goose spun around and saw her baby and she ran to him, scooping him up in her huge white wings and sobbed, "I thought you were gone, my sweet, sweet boy, I thought he'd eaten you!" She turned to Father Fox, but before she had a chance to open her beak, Mother Fox was in her face snarling, "Look at him!" she said menacingly, and she gestured in the direction of her half-naked husband.

"I'm so sorry," Mother Goose wept.

"Sorry won't cut it, lady," Mother Fox roared in her face. "And you lot!" she said, whipping around and looking viciously at the other Manor Farm Geese which sent them flapping and squawking in terror. "Look what you've done!"

Swooping in, Monty demanded calmly, "Right, I think it's time you call it a night." He gestured to the crowd of onlookers to go away. "Off with you, go on," he boomed as Mother Fox paced up and down, trying to control her fury. Glad to escape the Manor Farm, creatures gathered their young and fled the scene.

CHAPTER 24

Newcomers Move South

Monty watched the sunrise; he couldn't sleep after all the upset of the party. As the sun started to burn off the dew from the grass, he could see movements below in the garden, and his heart sank. Gradually, the sight of the newcomers trailing down the great lawn was clear to see. One by one, the families of Mice, Rabbits, Moles, Foxes, Ducks, Toads and Geese were followed by the tragic sight of Mother Hedgehog and her two children.

Silently taking to the air, he watched them trundle along until they reached the most southerly part of the garden. Resting on the branch of an oak tree, he saw the family of Grey Squirrels eager to greet them.

"Hey!" Brazil shouted to the young Rabbits, do you want to come and explore?"

"Give them a chance," his mother said. "They need to settle first."

"Great," Brazil said, jumping into action and addressing the Rabbits first. "I know all around here. I know the perfect place for you to stay. There's an empty burrow over there under that oak. It may need a little work, but it will keep you warm and safe this winter." Then turning to the ducks, he said, "There's a lovely spot by the river just on the bend where you will be safe."

"It may be a little noisy," his mother pointed to the swamp and smiled. "Our neighbors love to party." Right on cue, there was a big roar then a cheer followed by blood-chilling screams which sounded like a fight.

"What about us?" the Moles asked.

"Maybe you could go with the Ducks and look after each other?" Brazil suggested.

"And don't forget, no digging," Brazil's mother added. "Monty said we are not to upset the Humans."

Nodding, the Moles scampered off behind the Ducks, who were followed by the Toads.

Monty silently watched Brazil and his mother organise every creature until all that was left in front was Mother Hedgehog and her children.

"I think you should stay close to us," Brazil's mother suggested kindly to Mother Hedgehog.

"What about the hedge at the bottom of our tree?" Brazil suggested. Then, scurrying around the Grey Squirrel family, he foraged and found everything they needed to make the Hedgehog family comfortable in their new home.

With a heavy heart in silence, Monty cursed himself for failing the newcomers, and he flew away to sound the morning call.

CHAPTER 25

Autumn

After the frantic food collection for the winter was complete, it was now time to relax. The arrival of autumn brought a gentler pace of life to the garden and visitors lessened as the days grew shorter and the weather colder. The once-green leaves of many trees were changing to a spectrum of colours from vivid yellows to deep golds through to oranges and vibrant reds before gently falling to the ground.

Monty marveled at Mother Nature's display of beauty as he did his evening rounds. He thought of the migrating Birds readying for their long flight to a warmer climate and those preparing for their long winter sleep. He knew this was the last meeting the Geese and Swallows would attend until their return in the spring. He was always sad to see them go and worried for them on their long journeys. But he knew it was their way—they had to go. With the help of Mother Nature, they would all be back again next year.

It had been a couple of weeks since the newcomers had left their hosts' homes. From a distance, Monty had kept a watchful eye on them to make sure they were ok. He still hoped they would attend the evening meetings, or the creatures of the Great Garden would feel bad and invite them back. But landing on the bowling green for the evening meeting, he was disappointed yet again.

"Really," Mother Goose said, holding court, "and after all, we did for them. Mother Fox, wouldn't you agree?" But before Mother Fox had a chance to answer, she continued, "They came here to our home and ate our food without a word of thanks."

"And what about our winter stores?" Mother Badger added. "We worked long and hard."

"Come ladies," Monty interrupted, "we are not sure what happened to them."

"Manor Farm happened to them," Mother Fox snapped back, and Mother Badger nodded her head in agreement.

Wearily, Monty took his place at the front and scanned the crowd. He spotted Mother Squirrel scampering in with her three children but no Father Squirrel in sight. Monty cursed himself, he had failed them all.

CHAPTER 26

Winter in the garden

Winter quickly followed autumn, and Mother Squirrel's desperate need for sleep grew each day which told her winter had arrived, but sleep was a luxury she couldn't afford. Cuddled up with her family in their warm home, the thought of going out filled her with dread. She tried to go back to sleep, but her head raced. Round and round her thoughts swirled with a never-ending sense of doom.

All she could think about was how much trouble they were in, and she could see no way out. She looked across at Father Squirrel who had arrived home late again last night. She had no idea where he went, but he looked like a wreck. His once healthy, shiny red coat was matted with dirt, and he stank. Her heart broke as she wondered what had gone wrong. A tear ran down her face as she remembered how happy they once were.

Peeping out of their home high in the Canadian Oak, she saw the freezing fog of the November morning blocking the watery sunrise. She looked longingly back at her children who were curled up sleeping.

She wished with all her heart she could go back to them and sleep through the winter. But despite the fog, she could see the Holly Bush rustling below, and she knew she had to find the rats' food.

Checking their winter food store, she was shocked at how little they had left. A familiar knot of anxiety grew stronger in her stomach. They would never have enough food to see them through. But where was it going? She was puzzled. All the food she gave the Rat, she had foraged herself. With the Rat's growing appetite and their food mysteriously disappearing, she had no choice but to collect more and more. In a bid to keep her foraging missions a secret, she went to remote parts of the garden hoping nobody would see her. Each day, her search for food grew harder and took her further from home.

Heading to the south side of the garden, she figured it was a good place to gather food as only the newcomers lived there, and nobody would believe them if they said they'd seen her up and out. The further south she went the lonelier she felt and the closer she got to the swamp and the dreaded Rats and Minks. She was a long way from home. She hated this part of the garden, especially the strange smell of the rotting swamp which hung heavy in the freezing air. Desperate to get the food and get back to her bed, she figured if she got plenty it might keep the Rat going for a few days, and she might get some desperately needed sleep.

Rushing and unable to see over the pile of chestnuts in her arms, she tripped and found herself flying through the frosty air. Desperately clinging to her precious load, she came crashing to a heap on the frozen ground. Her aching muscles jarred on impact with the solid ground her arms took the biggest blow.

Sickened with the raging pain that flooded her body, she knew she was in trouble, alone, helpless, and a long way from home. She started to cry. Nothing in her life made sense. All she could see was a dark hole, and there was no way out. If she told the truth, her family would be kicked out of the garden, but she knew she couldn't sustain this.

Attempting to get up, she yelped out as the pain shot through her right arm. It was unbearable. She knew nobody would come looking for her because nobody knew she was there. Lonely sobs escaped her body, and once they started, she felt they would never end. She cried for her children; how would they survive if she didn't return?

CHAPTER 27

Brazil to the rescue

Brazil was having great fun checking the slippery surface of tree trunks. He would slide down one then dash back up and jump to the next species looking for the slipperiest one. A winter storm had ravaged the garden the night before, and his mother had asked him to check on the sleeping Hedgehog family. Seeing they had not stirred, he decided to have some fun.

He heard Mother Squirrel's cries but passed it off as his partying neighbors in the swamp. Then seeing a gimps of red fur on the frozen ground, he moved swiftly to investigate. Realising it was Mother Squirrel he wondered why she was awake as his father had told him Red Squirrels needed more sleep than them in the winter. He knew Grey Squirrels were forbidden to go near the red ones, but he could see this one was in trouble. Slowly, he moved closer and was shocked at how thin she looked.

"Can I help you?" he said softly, not wanting to frighten her. Mother Squirrel couldn't hear him over her sobs. "Excuse me," he said a little louder, but she still wailed, so he shouted, "Do you need any help?!"

Mother Squirrel jumped with fright increasing the level of pain in her right arm to a whole new level. "No, I am," she said through gritted teeth, "I am fine, I am fine." She tried to stand, but the pain was too much, and she fell back down to the ground, sobbing.

Brazil ventured closer and said gently, "If you don't mind me saying you don't look fine." Mother Squirrel stood up again and clutched her injured arm. In a very weak voice, she said, "I'm fine." Finally, she took a very slow, tiny step forward.

"Please!" he begged. "Let me help you."

"Sorry," she whimpered again. "Can't do that." She took another slow, agonising step. Seeing her in so much pain, he moved closer and said softly, "Please let me help you."

Mother Squirrel stopped and stared at him. A rush of thoughts muddled her brain: What would Father Squirrel say if he knew she'd been near a Grey Squirrel? How was she going to feed the Rat? What if she was found helping a Rat? Then, her desperate need to get home overwhelmed her. A whirlwind of thoughts whizzed through her brain, again and again. She couldn't breathe, and she felt dizzy.

"Breathe," Brazil said calmly, looking into her face. "Breathe, take a deep breath." But Mother Squirrel blurted back, "I don't have time for this. I must get home. I have so much to do!"

"That can wait!" he replied, which sent her into a complete frenzy.

"Wait! Wait!" she screeched through gritted teeth. "You have no idea. So many depend on me!"

He slowly reached out and took her tear-stained face in his paws. "Breathe" he repeated. "Take a deep breath." He looked straight into her eyes. As if hypnotised by Brazil's huge charcoal grey eyes, Mother Squirrel stopped talking and started to follow his instructions. "That's great," he said slowly, "nice deep, slow breaths. Fill your tummy full of air." Seeing her start to relax, he let go of her face and said, "Now, let me see how badly you're hurt."

"But I need the food," she started to panic again.

"Concentrate on your breathing," he replied. "That's great. Slow deep breaths and let me worry about the food. Now, do you think you can walk?" he asked. Concentrating hard on her breathing, Mother

Squirrel managed to take a tiny step and nodded. "That's great," he said, gathering up the nuts she'd dropped. "You walk, and I'll carry these, unless you need my help?" She smiled a weak smile at him. She was so grateful she had forgotten what it felt like to have somebody take care of her. Very slowly, they inched their way back to the old Canadian Oak tree.

The short winter day was nearly at an end as they drew closer to their destination. The closer she got, the more her head raced. What if Father Squirrel or any of the other creatures saw her with a Grey Squirrel? What if Brazil saw the Rat? What if the Rat... the thoughts started to clog her brain until she felt weak and dizzy again. Sensing her agitation growing, Brazil simply commanded, "Breathe, you're doing so well. Concentrate on your breath and notice it going in and out of your lungs. You are nearly home." He tried to console her.

"But what if...." she tried to argue, but he cut her off and said firmly, "The most important thing right now is we get you home warm and safe. The rest will take care of itself." She wished it was that simple and took a deep breath, filling her lungs with the crisp winter air.

As Brazil followed Mother Squirrel home, he couldn't help but wonder why she needed all the nuts. It had been a cold winter, and the Red Squirrels should have slept through most of it, not needing much food. They used their summer fat to see them through their long sleep. But he reckoned she looked far too thin to survive this winter. Something didn't add up.

CHAPTER 28

Mother Squirrel Reaching Home

It was nightfall as the Canadian Oak came into sight. Mother Squirrel had no idea how she was going to climb its tall tree trunk up to her home. She dreaded to think how angry the Rat was going to be with no food all day, and she didn't have to wait long to find out. As soon as she heard the rustle of the crisp leaves under their tree, the dreaded voice from Holly Bush started.

"Where have you been? We had a deal!" Mother Squirrel tried to cover up the voice by shouting at him, "Thanks, you have been a great help!" Then, she waved her good arm at Brazil to dismiss him and said coldly, "Now, off you go now."

"I just want to see you safely into your home," he insisted.

"No, you must go!" she commanded. "Father Squirrel will be furious if he sees you here." But Brazil was going nowhere. He was fascinated, and he wanted to know who owned the voice under the

Holly Bush. Putting the nuts down he helped Mother Squirrel creep slowly up the steep tree trunk.

Once she was safely inside, he jumped across to a neighboring tree and pretended to leave. Instead, he waited high in the canopy to see just who was hiding under the Holly Bush.

Mother Squirrel quietly entered her home. Everybody slept soundly. Conflicting emotions flooded her body. She felt relief to be home safe but sad knowing once spring came, her three children would be off finding their own mates and starting up their own families. What would she be left with? She looked at Father Squirrel snoring in the corner. The thought filled her with dread. She laid her exhausted aching body down and cuddled up behind her daughter Hazel for warmth. She had never felt so cold before. Exhaustion was greater than the pain in her body, and she instantly fell into the deepest sleep of her life.

CHAPTER 29

Brazil Meets Mother Rat

Brazil watched the Holly Bush and nearly gasped out loud when the big Rat made an appearance. Greedily, she scooped up the nuts and ran off, furtively looking over her shoulder to make sure she hadn't been seen. Brazil followed, jumping silently from tree to tree until finally the Rat stopped at an old, hollowed-out beech tree. Making one final check, she looked all around before disappearing through a small crack in the trunk. The old beech tree was dead from a lightning strike many years earlier, but its huge empty trunk still stood tall, defying the storms of recent years. Its state of decay meant it stunk, making it the perfect place for the Rat to hide as no other creatures wanted to live there. Plus, the rotting smell reminded her of her old home in the swamp. Jumping across to the top of the dead tree, Brazil heard the sound of delighted voices. Looking down its hollowed trunk, he could just barely make out the family of young Rats heartily devouring the nuts.

"So that's why you need so much food," Brazil said out loud. Mother Rat jumped and turned to the source of the voice. Looking up at the long hollow trunk, she could barely make out his shape in the dark. "Who are you? What do you want?" she shouted in terror.

"I could ask you the same," he replied. "I thought Rats weren't allowed in the Great Garden?"

"We're not," she sobbed feeling her cover was blown. She worried her family would be kicked out of the Great Garden. She pointed to her children, and ten innocent faces stared back at him. "I don't want them to grow up like those savages in the swamp. I want them to have respect for themselves and those around them." She wailed, "I wanted them to grow up surrounded by love not fear." She cried and fell into a heap, her heart breaking at the thought of them returning to the swamp.

Brazil climbed further down the rotting tree trunk to get a better look at Mother Rat. He was puzzled, "Why was Mother Squirrel helping you?" Mother Rat shifted from foot to foot. "I needed help, and she was the only one I could trust." She continued hanging her head in shame. "Well, I didn't really give her any choice. But!" she said quickly, "I was desperate. My babies needed feeding, and I couldn't be seen in the garden collecting food." Brazil perched quietly, processing what she said. "Please don't tell anybody," She pleaded, "I made her do it. I blackmailed her, and she's terrified she'll get kicked out too. Please tell her I'm so sorry."

Brazil thought, who was he to judge? He was himself a visitor and was lucky enough to winter in the Great Garden. But he was aware of the rules and didn't want to upset anybody. He also knew how much trouble Mother Squirrel would be in with the other creatures. Taking control, he said, "From now on, I'll bring your food, enough for all of you. I will feed you, and you let Mother Squirrel sleep. In fact, nobody must know that she ever helped you, is that clear?" he said sternly. Mother Rat slumped with relief. "Oh! Thank you, thank you, thank you!" she said in relief and gratitude.

"Oh!" he added, "the best way to teach your children how to be good creatures is to lead by example, and they will follow." As he shot up inside the tree trunk calling over his shoulder, "I'll be back in the morning."

CHAPTER 30

Hazel Wakes

The next morning, Hazel woke unexpectedly from her winter sleep. She registered the damp, cold feeling on her back and she turned to see her mother's mud-stained shivering body. Instantly, she knew she was unwell, and it was serious. Not knowing what to do, she thought of waking her father, but she feared he would wake in a terrible mood and be of no help. Sticking her head out of their home, she looked around frantically hoping to see somebody. Then she spotted Brazil on his way to feed the Rats.

"Help!" she cried, startling Brazil. He feared he'd been caught breaking the rules. Looking up, he saw what he could only describe as the most beautiful Squirrel that had ever roamed this earth. Her raven-red fur glistened in the winter sunlight. Mesmerised by her little fat cheeks, his brain didn't compute what she was saying. Frustrated with his lack of response, Hazel threw an acorn shell at him, and even though it bounced off his head, he didn't move. Wow, he thought approvingly, she's feisty too, his perfect kind of lady Squirrel.

Frustrated and in a panic, Hazel ran down the tree trunk and screamed into his face, "Help me!" Snapping out of his daze, Brazil realised this must be Mother Squirrel's daughter. Either they were a family of drama queens or maybe she was in trouble. Dragging him by the paw, she cried, "It's my mother, she won't wake up! Please help! I don't know what to do." Running up the Canadian Oak, he took one look at Mother Squirrel and said, "I'll go get help." Brazil caught her by the paw and said, "I'll fetch my mother she will know what to do." Then he darted out.

After what felt like hours to Hazel, Brazil and his mother burst into the home. Instantly assessing the situation, Brazil's mother said to Hazel, "Lie beside her and keep her warm."

Disorientated and bleary-eyed from days of sleeping, her brothers Cashew and Pecan woke and looked at each other in disbelief. They had been unceremoniously woken from their big winter sleep to find two Grey Squirrels in their home shouting orders at their sister. They jumped to their feet to defend their home from the evil invaders.

"Get out!" the brother Squirrels hissed at the Grey Squirrels. They lunged forward, their claws outreached. "Stop!" Hazel cried as Brazil dove forward to defend his mother then lassoed his long fluffy tail around their feet. He pulled hard, knocking the two brothers back to the ground. Cashew and Pecan lay on the floor, unsure of what had just happened, then Brazil's Mother screamed, "Look at your mother! She is very sick."

Father Squirrel, who had been disturbed by all the racket, lifted his head slowly and opened one eye. Then, convinced he was having a terrible nightmare, flipped over and went back to sleep to avoid the idea that Grey Squirrels would ever be in his home.

"Look!" Brazil's Mother invited Cashew and Pecan to look at their mother. Turning, they saw the shrunken, shivering body of their mother gasping for air through chattering teeth. "We are trying to help her," Brazil said to Pecan and Cashew as they registered the enormity of the situation.

"What can we do to help?" Pecan volunteered.

"We need dry leaves to wrap her in. We need to get her warm," Brazil's Mother said gently.

"Whatever you want," Cashew said as he flew out the door.

"And some food and water," she called after them, "she is woefully thin." Then, turning to Brazil, she said, "Comfrey leaves. There are still some growing down by the river. They will help with the swelling in her arm." Without another word, Brazil followed the two brothers out the door.

Everybody did as they were told that day and all through that night. Brazil's mother made poultices of mashed comfrey leaves and placed them on Mother Squirrel's injured body. She showed Hazel how to gently clean the mud from her mother's fur. She even managed to get Mother Squirrel to eat a little mashed food. She explained everything she was doing to Hazel and how it would aid her mother's recovery. After the first day passed, they could visibly see improvement. Her shivering had stopped, and she slept peacefully.

CHAPTER 31

Mother Squirrel Heals

As the days passed, Brazil and his mother became frequent visitors to the Red Squirrels' home. They brought food supplies, and Brazil's Mother praised Hazel for doing an excellent job. Over time, the two families talked, relaxed, and even laughed in each other's company, and soon, they saw no difference between them. They were all the same except Red Squirrels slept a lot more in the winter than grey and they had different colour fur. Cashew and Pecan had shown Brazil around the garden, and Brazil's mother taught Hazel how to look after the family in her mother's absence. All this took place whilst Father Squirrel slept in the far corner, only grunting his objections without even opening his eyes.

The family was exhausted after being awake in such cold weather, but they were glad they could help their mother. Every day she started to look more like her old self, and her children started to relax and get some sleep. It was whilst they were fast asleep one day that she woke with a start. How long have I been asleep? The Rat will be furious, she thought. Jumping up to go out in search of food, her home spun as she felt dizzy. Standing still to steady herself, she looked down and noticed her shiny red coat. She was puzzled, where had all the mud gone? Then, she moved her injured arm. Miraculously it moved and there was no pain. Puzzled, had she imagined falling and hurting herself? Then, panic set in instantly as she remembered the Rat again.

Sensing her mother move, Hazel awoke. Delighted to see her mother awake she jumped to her feet and called out to her brothers. The three young squirrels surrounded their mother ecstatic to have her back. Confused, shocked and not used to displays of affection, Mother Squirrel tried to break free of them. "Stop! I have things to do," she protested. "Please let me go." But her children were having none of it.

"Go where?" Hazel questioned. "We just got you back and we don't intend to let you go anywhere. Sit! Whatever it is, we can get it for you." Hazel's brothers agreed.

Mother Squirrel jumped when Brazil's face appeared in their doorway. Brazil winked at her, then he grinned a big smile. "No need to worry. Your job's taken care of, and everybody is happy."

She realised he must have heard the Rat under the Holly Bush. She started to panic; how did she know she could trust him? Wanting to go out and see for herself, she tried to wriggle from her children's embrace. She was startled once more when Brazil's Mother also appeared in the opening.

"You're a sight for sore eyes!" Brazil's Mother said, smiling. They all laughed, cheered, and danced around Mother Squirrel, nearly smothering her. There was a grunt from a sleeping Father Squirrel in the corner which sent Mother Squirrel into a panic, fearing he would wake and find Grey Squirrels in his home.

Sensing her distress, Brazil's Mother led her gently to bed, whispering so as not to further disturb Father Squirrel. "You lie down there and rest. You need to build your strength up and let us take care of the rest." Mother Squirrel was happy to lay her dizzy head down—just the effort of standing had taken it out of her. She would do as they said, and when they were all back asleep, she would slip out.

"You lay down there," Brazil's Mother said. "We don't want you getting sick again, do we?" But just as Mother Squirrel went to lay her head back down, her mouth dropped open in shock to see Father Squirrel staring back at her. Terror gripped her body as her eyes bulged in her head. Seeing her distress, the children followed her stare, and the atmosphere in the house changed.

"What on earth?" he boomed, jumping to his feet to face Brazil and his mother. He roared, "Get out you filthy, dirty, rotten creatures! Get out of my home!"

Brazil tried to shield his mother from the attack, but Father Squirrel's rage choked the room. He continued his tirade of abuse. "I know you lot were scum, but really, I can't believe you're in my home! I'll have you thrown out of the garden! Your type should never have been let in."

The three young Red Squirrels stood in front of their father to protect their newly found friends.

"Please Pops," they pleaded, "they helped us. They are our friends." Father Squirrel stood with his mouth open in complete shock. This was the ultimate betrayal—his own family turning against him. How could they be so stupid, so weak, so gullible, to fall for the lies of these nasty Red Squirrels.

Not able to contain his rage and afraid of what he might do, he shot out the door barely touching the tree trunk, in search of relief from the consuming rage which threatened to smother him.

CHAPTER 32

Spud

As winter rolled on Spud thought she might die of boredom. She hated winter. She was tired watching Radish and Grandpa sleeping all day in the burrow. She felt so lonely, and she craved some excitement. Lost in her misery, she jumped when she heard a voice say: "Hey!" Unable to see anyone, she looked around and found Father Squirrel lying flat on his back in the frozen undergrowth.

"Help me?" he asked cheerily. "My legs don't seem to work," he said bursting out into uncontrollable laughter.

Spud was shocked at Father Squirrel's appearance. He looked wretched. His shiny coat and fluffy tail were matted and dirty, and he stank. His once chubby body was just skin and bones, but despite all that, he was so happy.

Father Squirrel held out his hand to Spud and demanded, "Come, help me up!" Spud obeyed, lifting Father Squirrel onto her back, and they set off in the direction of his home. Reaching the Canadian Oak, they met Mother Squirrel.

"I had a lovely time," Father Squirrel slurred, smiling when he saw her. "Great fun with my friends!" he said spitefully in her direction.

Mother Squirrel called to her sons, "Pecan, Cashew, your father needs some help." Instantly, her boys were at her side. Together, they skillfully lifted Father Squirrel from Spud's back and dragged him up the tree trunk. "Thank you, my friend," Father Squirrel shouted over his shoulder to Spud.

"Now off you go, off you go," Mother Squirrel said abruptly, waving her hands at Spud. She paced up and down until Spud was out of sight then turned and ran up the tree to Father Squirrel. "What are you doing?" she said angrily into his face. "You will get us kicked out of the garden!"

"You worry too much," Father Squirrel replied. Then, he roared laughing into her face as she danced around with frustration, fury, anger, and fear.

CHAPTER 33

Later that Day

The watery morning sun gave the illusion of heat as Spud lay shivering in the long grass near the Canadian Oak. She was curious, and she wanted to know what had made Father Squirrel so happy. Who were these friends he'd had so much fun with? Spud was delighted when Leek appeared. "What are you up to?" she asked, hoping for something to do but as usual was terrified of what Spud might suggest.

"Shush! Get down," Spud gestured to Leek, "I'm waiting for Father Squirrel. He's up to something, and I want to know what." They both ducked down just as Father Squirrel appeared at the top of the Canadian Oak.

"Gosh," Leek mumbled, shocked to see the skeleton figure of this once great Squirrel.

"Shush," Spud glared at her to be quiet.

Father Squirrel inched slowly down the tree trunk; his hollow cheeks frantically billowed with the effort. Little groans of pain escaped his tight lips. Finally reaching the forest floor, he disappeared into the long, shiny grass and was only visible by his raggedy tail and the odd pop of his head checking to see that nobody was following him. The two young Rabbits watched him go to his family's winter food store. Then, with as much food as he could physically carry, he hobbled away, heading south. Watching from a distance, Spud and Leek gasped as they watched Father Squirrel cross the river by a fallen tree then stagger down the narrow path and disappear into the swamp.

CHAPTER 34

The Swamp

Spud bounded forward hot on Father Squirrels trail. "Stop!" Leek hissed, "We can't! We mustn't!" But Spud's desire to know what the swamp was like and why they were forbidden to go there was too strong. She'd heard the stories, but she had to find out for herself. "You can stay here if you want, but I am going," she said firmly to Leek.

Leek watched in horror as Spud scampered over the fallen tree that spanned the river and disappeared down the same path. She began to panic. Leek had heard stories from her parents of creatures who went into the swamp and were never seen again. She loved Spud like a sister, and she couldn't bear the thought of losing her, so she reluctantly followed.

The path narrowed once clear of the fallen tree that marked the start of the swamp. The morning frost was starting to melt and drops fell from the trees making Leek jump every time one landed on her. A heavy mist hovered over the flooded land, and the stink of rotting vegetation filled the air which made Leek feel sick. Leek soon realised this place was worse than she'd imagined. The tightly clumped trees with their heavy canopy made it so dark that it felt more like night. They listened for danger with all their senses on high alert as they slowly moved deeper into the swamp.

Black plastic bags of human rubbish were slung everywhere, bottles floated on the dead murky water whilst used baby nappies were closer to its edge. The bags had been ripped open and their multi-coloured content was scattered everywhere. They passed an old car disintegrating into the putrid landscape, and its rainbow-coloured oil shimmered on the surface of the swamp making it the blackest water Leek had ever seen. Sneaking in behind a higgledy-piggledy pile of old tires. Leek gasped with horror as they watched as Father Squirrel was welcomed by the Rats and minks and Spud shot her a look that told her to be quiet.

The Minks and Rats were a tough-looking lot, each covered in battle scars, missing ears, and scarred faces, a testimony to the tough life they lived. Spud and Leek silently watched as Father Squirrel handed over the food.

"Is that all?" the meanest-looking rat said menacingly into Father Squirrel's face.

"That's all I could carry!" Father Squirrel tried to reason.

"That's your problem," the head Rat boomed back at him. "If you want the goods, you'll have to pay for it."

"Please!" Father Squirrel pleaded. "I'll do anything you ask."

"Remember that" the head rat said viciously poking Father Squirrel into his chest, "just you remember that." Then, he clapped his paws and Father Squirrel was led over to a heavily guarded plant with a large white flower. Spud and Leek watched fascinated as Father Squirrel hobbled close to it then gently grasping its delicate petals in his shaking paws, he took a gigantic sniff. Seconds later gone was his limped; instead, he danced around like a young Squirrel full of life. Happily, he leapt and jumped around, making the Rats and Minks laugh. It reminded Spud of the Harvest Party, and right now, he desperately wanted some fun and to be as happy as Father Squirrel.

Leek, on the other hand, was shaking, horrified by what she saw. Whilst Father Squirrel danced and sang, the Minks and Rats greedily grabbed at the food he'd brought. "You got more than me!" a nasty looking Mink said to a Rat standing beside him. Suddenly, a vicious fight broke out.

"We need to leave," Leek pleaded anxiously pulling at Spud just as a deep chilling voice from behind them said, "Nobody is going anywhere."

Spud and Leek slowly turned around to find dozens of terrifying minxes staring back at them.

The stood opened mouthed until finally, Spud managed to squeak out, "Looks like you're having a party."

"Yeah! You want to join the fun?" the largest, meanest Mink croaked. Spud nodded despite her terror. She was fed up, always feeling sad about her mum and brother; she wanted to feel happy like Father Squirrel. In a cackling voice, the meanest Mink said, "Come" and he led the way to the water's edge where the party was in full swing.

While Spud followed the Mink, Leek remained frozen to the spot. Her eyes desperately darted around looking for an escape route, but she didn't know these woods and knew if she tried to run, she would get lost and be captured.

"You coming? Or do I have to make ya!" one of the Minx snapped. Leek stepped forward about to follow when she spotted a paw from the undergrowth signaling to her. Then, a large Rat appeared and mouthed, "Follow me." Leek rubbed her eyes, convinced she was imagining things.

One of the Minks looked back, and the Rat instantly disappeared. Seeing Leek rub her eyes, a Mink jibed, "Oh diddums', are we crying?" Then, he ordered her to, "Move it! We haven't got all day."

Leek reluctantly started to move in the direction of the party when she spotted the Rat again frantically waving at her to follow. Reckoning she had nothing to lose, she darted under the bush and ran like the wind after the Rat. Behind her, she could hear the cries of the Minks as they started to chase them, but she clearly had an excellent guide. They flew under the bushes, up a small stream, and slid down a fallen tree trunk towards freedom.

Soon, they were clear of the swamp and in an open grassland near the back of the Great Garden when the Rat finally stopped.

"Thank you," Leek gasped breathlessly.

"No time for that," she gasped back, "your friend and the Squirrel are in real danger. You need to get help and quick!"

Realising she was right, Leek bounded off for Grandpa Rabbit's burrow.

CHAPTER 35

Leek Goes for Help

Leek burst into the burrow to find Radish and Grandpa Rabbit curled up, having an afternoon nap. "Spud's in trouble!" she yelled. Then, gasping for breath, she added, "You must come, quick!"

Being hard of hearing, Grandpa shouted at Radish, "What's she saying?" But he didn't answer. Instead, Leek yelled into Grandpa's face, "Spud's in big trouble! The Minks have her in the swamp. I need your help, come quick." Then, she turned and ran out of the burrow followed by Radish and Grandpa.

"It's no use," Grandpa puffed, "I can't keep up." Radish and Leek slowly disappeared into the distance as he shouted, "You go. I'll get Monty!"

They soon reached the fallen tree, and Leek stopped and looked at Radish. "Are you sure you want to do this?" and he nodded, eyes wide open in terror. His sister needed him, and he wasn't prepared to lose her as well. "Ok, from now on, we need to be very quiet." Together, they tiptoed into the swamp.

Following the sounds of the revelers, they made their way to the platform where they hid before. They could see Father Squirrel still dancing around and acting silly amongst the Rats and Minx. Then, Spud came into view. She was pleading with them to let her have what Father Squirrel had.

"Yes, yes, all in good time," the leader of the Minks said, "but first we need to talk business. What do we get out of it?"

"Anything, you name it!" Spud said impatiently. She wanted to be as happy as Father Squirrel.

"I hear you can get tomatoes," Morris the head Mink said, licking his lips.

"Yes!" The other Rats and Minks roared with excitement.

"Yep, no problem," Spud said cockily. Then pausing, she questioned, "But how do you know that?"

"I know everything," he said into her face. "I know everything." He howled laughing.

"I'll get you some tomatoes," Spud agreed, and they sealed the deal by slapping paws. "Now, please give me a smell?" Morris nodded his approval, and a rat ran forward flower and just as she prepared to take a deep breath Radish screamed, "No!!!" Leek flipped into the air with fright and Spud spun around, and Radish yelled again, "No! Don't do it!" Seeing her brother's way in the distance, she smiled. This was instantly replaced with panic as she watched the Minks dash up to the bank to get them.

"Run!" she screamed at them. "Run for your lives!" But it was too late. They were captured and marched down to the main party with no chance of escape this time.

Reunited, the three young Rabbits clung to each other for comfort. They were heavily surrounded by very angry Minks and Rats who circled them and loudly discussed the nasty ways they would punish them. Radish closed his eyes and prayed they would find a way out of this. "I'm so sorry," Spud sobbed through chattering teeth. "This is all my fault."

"Stop!" Radish said it more optimistically than he felt. "We're not done for yet."

Standing on their hind legs, they clung tightly to each other, locked in fear. They pressed their heads together in a vain attempt to block out the crazy noises around them. They pressed even harder when they heard wild whooping and screams filling the air, then even harder when they felt things hitting off their bodies.

"Think happy thoughts!" Leek shouted.

"What!" Spud cried "With all this going on?"

"Do it! Imagine us, home and safe with your grandpa," Leek hollered over the noise.

"No time for that!" Spud screamed.

"Do it! Imagine us all sitting in the burrow with lots of food, and Grandpa's telling us stories of your Mamma when she was little."

"How is this going to help?" Radish shook.

"Please just do it! Really imagine it. Remember how it will feel and smell and look like please," She pressed her head even harder against theirs. "Focus on what we want, not what we fear is about to happen."

"But there is no way out!" Spud sniveled.

"No buts!" Leek said crossly. "Believe we are there tonight safe with Grandpa."

"Ok, I'll try," Spud whispered.

CHAPTER 36

Minding their own business

The gardeners called the southerly part of the garden their wild garden, but to the untrained eye, it looked neglected and particularly bleak at this time of year. It was a place where Mother Nature was allowed to do her own thing, and it was easy to forget you were in a garden. Brazil was out searching for food for Mother Rat and her growing brood. Foraging between the long-matted grasses he felt a slight tremor in the crisp soil beneath his feet. Carefully put down the nuts sensing something was wrong Brazil bobbed down in the long grass. The wind grew with his fear as the tremor turned to a rumble. The tree branches rustled slightly, and the sky shaded over as a cavalcade of creatures stampeded past him.

Dozens of Rabbits propelled by powerful hind legs flew through the air. Mice clung to the backs of Foxes, holding on for dear life. Overhead, flashes of Red Squirrels flew through the branches, and the murky sky darkened with a dense flock of Birds of every variety. All were led by Monty and Horus.

Instinctively, Brazil flew up into a tree and called out to the other newcomers, "lets follow." It was obvious this was a task force on a war mission, and from the direction they travelled in, it was clear the war was with the Rats and Minks.

Just as Brazil was about to leap off in pursuit came a yell, "Stop! Where do you think you're going?" Onions, a newcomer Rabbit, shouted at him.

"To Help!" Brazil said turning to leap to another tree after them.

Wanting to know what all the commotion was about, other sleepy newcomers appeared from their homes.

"The creatures of the Great Garden are in trouble!" Brazil cried.

"That's their problem," the head Badger grumbled, not happy being woken up.

"We have to help," Brazil reasoned. "They helped us when we needed it!" Then, he disappeared into the distance.

Quickly looking at each other and without further discussion, they realised he was right, and took off in pursuit.

CHAPTER 37

The Battle

Spud struggled at first to block out the terrifying noises that surrounded them. She imagined her grandpa's face and the telling off they would get when he got home. She didn't care as long as Leek and Radish were safe. She pictured them laughing and Radish telling Grandpa what an idiot she was.

Leek pictured in her mind all the things they were going to do when they were home. She had no idea how they were going to get there, she just trusted, really trusted, they would.

Just as Leek was losing herself in her thoughts, she felt a violent tugging at her tail. Ignoring it, she fought to stay with her happy thoughts, but it became more forceful, and she could feel herself being dragged away from the others. Opening one eye, she was startled to see the big Rat who had helped her earlier. She shouted at her, but Leek couldn't hear over the dim. Opening her other eye, Leek saw the biggest battle happening—unlike anything she had ever seen.

"Look! Look!" Leek screamed at Spud and Radish. Slowly opening their eyes, they saw dozens of swooping Birds dive-bombing the Rats and Minks, their sharp talons outstretched, whilst Red and Grey Squirrels hung from branches above, bombarding them with pinecones, nut shells, and anything they could find. Badgers, Foxes and Rabbits stood high on the bank, cascading rocks, and boulders in their direction.

"Quick, follow me!" the Rat yelled. Leek obeyed, but Radish and Spud hesitated and feared this was a trap. Running back to them, Leek yelled, "It's ok, you can trust her." Then, she dragged them after her.

They ran as fast as they could despite the constant deluge of acorn shells branches, rocks, and stones, raining from above. Reaching a clearing, Leek stopped and shouted, "I have to go back."

"No!" Radish wailed.

"I'm sorry. I can't leave Father Squirrel there. You follow the Rat. I know the way out. I'll catch up to you." Not listening to Radish's protests, she ran straight back into the action.

Leek returned to the battle ground and found Father Squirrel curled up in a tiny ball, hiding in a rotting log. She shouted, "Quick follow me!" They dove for cover as, yet another boulder crashed, narrowly missing them. Seizing their chance, Leek threw Father Squirrel on her back and escaped through the now familiar route.

Leek caught up with the others just as they re-entered the Great Garden to meet Grandpa Rabbit hobbling towards them. Tears of relief ran down his face as he held out his paws and they all ran to him. He was so relieved to see them and held them tight, savoring the moment.

Breaking from his grip, Spud blurted out excitedly, "Radish spoke! He did! He really did!" Then, she begged her brother, "Do it again, go on, do it again!"

"Give him a chance," Leek laughed, and Grandpa Rabbit held Radish's face in his paws; something had changed. His haunted vacant look was replaced with a weak smile as tears welled up in his eyes.

"That's my boy lets it out." Grand Pa Rabbit said hugging him tight to him as soft tears trickled down Radishes face quickly followed by a torrent of tears he didn't think would ever stop. Grandpa said gently still holding him tight, "Come on, son, let's get you home."

CHAPTER 38

The Trail of Father Squirrel

That very same night, Monty called an emergency meeting. He wanted to be sure everybody involved in the rescue mission was home safe. He also wanted to work out how they were going to punish Father Squirrel, Leek, and Spud.

Trying to contain his fury, Monty paced up and down the amphitheater in front of them. Eventually feeling calm enough to speak, he said, "So, were do we go from here?" He pointed his wing at the three creatures who stood in front of them, their heads all hung in shame.

"Can't see what all the fuss is about," Father Fox said still buzzing from the action. "That was the most excitement I've had in months."

"Yeah, it was brilliant!" Father Badger quickly agreed, "And those newcomers… they can really scrap."

"Yea!" Father Fox agreed laughing.

"I was so glad to see them," Mother Goose clucked.

Monty turned his back to the crowd and curled in a tight ball. The chatter stopped and the crowd fell into silence. Then spinning around, unable to hold his fury any longer, Monty exploded. His huge wings flew out, sending smaller creatures in the front row flying. "Excitement! Fun!" He danced around on the spot with his beak clamped shut trying to restrain himself, but it was no use.

"Fun! Fun! You have no idea what we've done!" he roared. "We had an agreement with the Rats and Minks. They live their lives their way in the swamp, and we do the same in the garden. Don't you get it? We attacked them in their home, and now, they will attack us back."

"They wouldn't dare," Father Badger chuckled. "They would have to get past the newcomers first," and they all roared laughing.

Monty screamed and stamped his feet, "Why can't you see how serious this is! We attacked them in their home. They will want payback. This is all out war." Silence fell whilst everybody took in the enormity of his statement.

Then, a quite whispered came from Father Squirrel "No they want."

Everybody looked at his withered trembling form with his head hung.

"Continue," Monty commanded.

"The night the newcomers moved in," Father Squirrel whispered and paused. "That was me," he sobbed, "I wanted you to think it was the newcomers, so you'd send them back." Then, he collapsed to his knees and continued weeping. The other creatures stared at him in stunned silence.

"So, that's how they knew about the tomatoes," Spud said, breaking the silence.

"Continue," Monty sternly prompted Father Squirrel.

"I just wanted them to make a mess, but once I let them in, I couldn't stop them. I showed them the food gathered for the party." Tears ran down his hollow cheeks, and he wiped his nose on his arm before continuing. "Then they forced me to show them your winter food stores. They threatened. If I didn't help them get food, they'd tell you what I did." He gulped again and looked at Mother Squirrel and his three offspring. "I couldn't have you thrown out of the garden because of my stupidity."

Time stood still in the garden as the creatures tried to absorb what he just told them. They watched him full of sadness, all remembering the great Squirrel he once was.

"And you're partying?" Monty's voice broke into their thoughts.

Father Squirrel rubbed his eyes and lifted his head slightly. "I couldn't live with what I'd done. I was so angry with you for letting the newcomers in, I couldn't bear to see any of you. I hated what I'd become, and I needed to escape my guilt. That was the only way I knew how." Fresh tears dripped off his dirty, matted fur.

Mixed emotions flooded through the crowd. First relief—they finally had the answer to who trashed the garden. But a heavy weight of guilt filled the air when they thought of how they had treated the newcomers.

CHAPTER 39

The Verdict

Later that evening, the creatures entered the amphitheater somberly, ready to tell Father Squirrel his fate. The Squirrel family stood alone on the highest point of the bank for all to see. Mother Squirrel had one hand firmly clasped over her mouth in the hope it would prevent her from being sick; her other hand was tightly wrapped around her three babies. Father Squirrel, who was a sad, lonely sight stood a little distance away, hung his head permanently in shame.

The creatures had taken all afternoon deliberating the fate of the Squirrel family, and Father Fox had volunteered to deliver it.

"As you know, Father Fox began, prancing up and down in front of the crowd enjoying his moment of responsibility. "We are gathered here to decide what will become of these creatures." Then he stopped and glared at the Squirrel family making Mother Squirrel muffle a sob.

"Get on with it," Monty snapped, losing his patience.

"I was getting to it," Father Fox said irritably as he cleared his throat and announced, "Father Squirrel, we have decided," he moved closer to his face, "to give you one more chance, but I am warning you," and he leaned menacingly against Father Squirrel's face, "if you are ever caught going near the swamp again, you will all be out! Banished from the garden forever." With that, Father Fox flounced off and Mother Squirrel collapsed in a heap and wept, and the onlookers assumed they were tears of relief, but she was still sick to her stomach, terrified they'd find out she helped the Rat.

"Right," Monty squawked to get everybody's attention. "In light of what we have heard today, I want to know how we are going to make it up to the newcomers."

There was a long silence as they all reflected on how they had treated the newcomers. Then muttering broke into discussions amongst themselves on how they could put it right. Eventually, Grandpa Rabbit said, "We only know one way to say sorry, and that is with food."

Rushing around to gather what little food they could spare from their meagre supplies the creatures headed out in the dark to the south side of the garden. Reaching the clearing behind the Pavilion, they laid it out on the ground.

Taking charge of the proceedings Monty called the Newcomers to join them. "We come in peace." His voice was muffled through the black, frosty air. When nobody appeared, he squawked louder. Gradually one by one, they could sense creatures all around them.

"We can never thank you for today, but more importantly we have come to say sorry." Monty bellowed into the darkness.

"We got it so terribly wrong," Father Badger echoed.

The rustling continued as outlines of faces emerged from the long grass.

"Sorry for what?" A Rabbit shouted from his hiding place.

"We know you didn't destroy our food," Monty said apologetically. We now know it was the Swam creatures."

Slowly more creatures appeared almost ghost-like through the freezing mist.

"We would like to apologise for the terrible way we treated you," Monty continued.

"And what happens the next time something goes wrong? "One of the newcomer Geese clucked.

"We all make mistakes," Father Fox said then turned to lick one of his bald patches.

"You all think you're better than us," another voice shouted from the dark.

"We just wanted to be friends," the Mice chorused together, "we are truly sorry.

A collective of Newcomers moved forward into sight, then a badger assuming the role of spokesperson said, "What about the Grey Squirrels? Just because the colour of their fur is different, doesn't mean they should be treated differently.

"Absolutely!" Monty nodded, "our apology extends to everyone, especially the Grey Squirrel family, they proved it today with their selflessness and courage and they are welcome anywhere in the Great Garden."

Brazil moved into sight and replied calmly "But we shouldn't have had to prove it" and a silence fell as shame hung heavy in the night air.

Breaking the silence Brazil said looking at all the food laid out in front of him, "thank you for the food".

"And for allowing us to move into your garden," his mother added standing beside him. Nods of appreciation then a chorus of thanks came from the Newcomers. Sensing that was as much as they could do for now, the Creatures of the Great Garden made their way home, wondering how they could ever make the newcomers feel welcome.

CHAPTER 40

The White Blanket

The residents woke the next morning to find a white blanket covering the garden. Excited young Birds, who had never seen snow before, tried to catch snowflakes in their beaks, Rabbits dove through high snow drifts, and Ducks skated clumsily across the ice on the lake whilst parents watched in amusement.

Monty wasn't feeling so full of life. The battle the day before and the freezing weather was really taking its toll on his tired old body. He sat high in his nest and wished for the first time that he didn't have to do his morning rounds. He knew there would be no visitors to the garden today and guessed the gardeners would be huddled in their greenhouse drinking hot tea, but he couldn't take the chance one of them would see them.

Spotting Horus flying beneath him, he shouted, "Isn't it about time you pull your weight around here?"

Looking up, Horus spied Monty in his nest and flew up to join him.

"Everything ok?" Horus enquired.

"Yes, yes of course it is!" Monty snapped defensively. "I just thought it about time you started shouldering some of the responsibilities around here."

"Whatever you need, Boss," Horus said, lifting his head proudly, delighted to be asked.

Full of pride Horus instantly set out on his rounds, familiar with the route he had seen Monty do it many times. Flying over the garden on his way home to his nest in the long rushes by the lake, Horus spotted Brazil flying through the trees, a long way from home. Puzzled by his behavior, Horus swooped down for a closer look and saw Brazil carrying food to an old burnt-out tree. Quietly landing on the top of the tree, Horis peered down into its hollowed-out trunk and was horrified to see the Rat and her young family happily tucking into the food below. "What on earth!" Horus boomed down the tree trunk, making Brazil and Mother Rat jump clean off the ground. "What on earth do you think you are doing? You know the rules."

Horus screeched so loud other creatures started appearing, wanting to know what all the fuss was about. "Rats!" Mother Fox yelled in horror as she wrapped her big, bushy tail around her cubs as if to protect them. More and more creatures gathered. "This is an outrage, young man," Horus shouted at Brazil. "You know how we feel about Rats."

Mother Goose scolded Brazil, "We were good enough to give you a home in your time of need, and this is how you repay us."

Mother Rat tried to defend Brazil, "It's not his fault," she cried but the other creatures were having none of it. "Get out!" the Ducks hissed. "Get out of our garden."

"Yes!" the Foxes joined in. "Get out! Go back to where you belong." Mother Rat stood in front of her babies attempting to shield them from abuse as more and more creatures gathered around them.

Unable to ignore the fuss, Monty flew in to see what was happening. "Please," he said irritably, "what is all the noise about?" The crowd parted to reveal Mother Rat and her brood of babies. "What on earth is going on here," he said in confusion.

Distracted from playing in the snow, Spud, Leek, and Radish followed the direction of the commotion. They pushed their way to the front to see what the fuss was about. Seeing Mother Rat cowering in front of her children, Leek shouted, "Stop! What are you doing? This is the Rat that saved us yesterday. She risked her own life getting us out of the swamp twice! She's the only reason we all made it out alive." The crowd silenced and looked at the Rat.

"Is that true?" Monty asked Mother Rat. Slowly lifting her head, she nodded.

"But why are you here?" he asked.

"I don't want to live in the swamp," she said shaking. "I want more for my children. I want them to grow up to be decent creatures away from all that mad partying and fighting."

"So, you thought you'd come here?" Monty said understandingly.

"Yes, I love the way you all look out for each other. I just wanted my children to grow up in a world like this."

"But why weren't you honest enough to come and ask us?" Monty enquired.

She was silent for a while, then replied, "My babies were on the way. I was desperate, and I needed to get out of there. You have seen what it is like, and I didn't think you would let me."

Monty searched around the crowd of onlookers. They were calmer now, starting to see her as another creature, not as the enemy.

"Tell us why we should trust you when every Rat we ever met has been untrustworthy?" Monty probed.

"I'm different, I promise," she pleaded. "Please let us stay. We can't go back. They will be so angry with me for helping you yesterday."

"Well, what do you think?" Monty slowly turned to look at the crowd.

"They must stay!" Leek shouted quickly, followed by Spud and Radish.

A mumbling started in the crowd that grew with momentum. Eventually, Father Fox stepped forward as the spokesperson. "They can stay, but we will be keeping a very close eye on you." He directed his words towards Mother Rat, "And don't think you can sneak any more of your sort into the garden."

"My sort!" Mother Rat said indignantly.

Father Fox turned on his heels and faced her. "Do you have a problem with that?" he said slowly.

"No, I mean, thank you. I promise, you won't be sorry," she said bowing humbly to him.

CHAPTER 41

Spring

The garden gently woke from its winter slumber. Bulbs poked their heads from the soil then burst into life, showering the garden floor with a carpet of purple, white, and yellow flowers. Pink and white blossoms and sticky green buds multiplied daily on the trees.

Spud sat alone under the oak tree watching the migrating birds return from their winter travels. As the sun gradually warmed the air, hibernating creatures woke to a love-filled garden with everybody either in search of a mate or busy extending their homes to get ready for new additions to their families. She was puzzled to see Mother and Father Fox being curiously kind to each other.

Surrounded by all this happiness made Spud miserable. She turned her head in disgust as Leek and Radish came into sight playfully feeding each other spring flowers.

Reading her thoughts, Grandpa Rabbit said as he slowly approached, "Spud, Be happy for them."

Then, catching his breath, he continued, "Never begrudge anyone their happiness." Spud looked at him with tears in her eyes, "But I just got him back." A big tear rolled down her cheek as she said, "and I've lost my best friend too."

"You haven't lost them. Look they are still there, and look," he pointed with his twitching nose to all the young Rabbits having great fun in the spring sunshine, "look at all the new friends you have yet to make." Gently he nudged her with his nose and reluctantly Spud moved towards them.

Turning back to the burrow for a nap, Grandpa Rabbit saw Mother Hedgehog sitting on her own. He wished her problems were as easily fixed. He could see many male Hedgehogs hovering around her, but she sat staring at the ground with the pain of grief etched on her face.

CHAPTER 42

Monty

Monty wasn't full of the joys of spring. His large, black wings felt much heavier than usual, the slightest move filled him with pain. He knew he was getting old, and the winter had been hard, and he wondered how many more springs he would see.

Rising early to ease the pain in his wings, he flew over the garden and counted his blessings. He thanked Mother Nature for his amazing life. Soaring in the clear blue sky giving his wings a good stretch out, he spotted young Hazel flying gracefully through the trees below him, her vibrant red coat contrasting against the young, green leaves and the pink and white blossoms. Then, his heart sank when he spotted the silver-grey coat of Brazil in hot pursuit, and he feared how Father Squirrel would react.

Father Squirrel hadn't been seen out since the night of his trial. Monty figured his poor tired body would need all the rest it could get after all his excessive partying. His thoughts were distracted as he flew over the great lawn and spotted Spud doing mighty back flips to the delight of a dozen young male Rabbits, all vying for her attention. By the river, he saw Mother Rat with her 10 beautifully behaved children following her down for a swimming lesson. He smiled to himself. It gave him great pleasure to see everybody getting along so well, but he still had an air of sadness at the thought of the newcomers still living in isolation.

CHAPTER 43

The Lake of Truth

Father Squirrel finally woke from his long, healing winter sleep. Looking around his empty home, he feared his family had left him. He lay for a while in silence and solitude, and the memories of what he had done filled his head. His heart was so heavy, and his body ached like never before, but he knew he had to try to put things right.

Easing himself down the long trunk of the Canadian Oak, he wandered aimlessly, ducking out of sight of other creatures. Eventually, he found himself at the water's edge of the Lake of Truth. He stood on the grassy bank, terrified to look into its still waters and see what he had become. He hoped taking a long, hard look at his reflection would help him work out what he had to do to make things right.

Slowly, he crept forward, and piece by piece his reflection appeared. First, his pointed ears, slowly followed by tired bloodshot eyes. Patches of matted, filthy fur entered the picture, until finally, stood in front of him was a squirrel he didn't recognise. Standing in his own pain he wondered where his youth had gone and how he'd got it all so wrong.

A lone tear ran down his hollow cheeks and dripped into the water fracturing his image as ripples moved out into the lake as more salty tears followed. He felt sick when he thought about stealing everyone's winter food and causing such trouble for the newcomers. He was disgusted with himself. How did it come to this?

He doubted his family would ever forgive him. He had been so caught up in his own rage and fear of the Grey Squirrels, he had thrown away the most important thing to him—his beautiful family. In his misguided quest to protect them, he had instead driven them all away.

As darkness came, he slowly made his way back to the Canadian Oak. Peering in the entrance of his home, he saw the back of Brazil and his mother standing over Mother Squirrel.

"That's right, take nice deep breaths," Brazil's Mother instructed Mother Squirrel. He watched in horror as Mother Squirrel gasped for air. Following their instructions, Mother Squirrel started to relax, and her breathing returned to normal. "What happened?" Brazil asked her. "You were doing so well. What upset you so?"

Mother Squirrel quietly gasped, "I came home and no Father Squirrel… I'm terrified he's gone to swamp!" As panicked reignited, her breathing became more rapid and shallow. "If he does, we'll be out …out of the garden for sure!"

"Don't you worry yourself about that. Brazil can go look for him". Brazil's Mother said trying to comfort her.

"No need," Father Squirrel said sheepishly from the opening. "That is one thing you'll never have to worry about again," he gulped through tears. Brazil and his mother jumped back afraid of Father Squirrel's reaction, but seeing his demeanor, they realised they had nothing to fear. Slowly moving toward Mother Squirrel, he promised, "I will never go there again."

Sensing the Grey Squirrels' discomfort, he said, "I can't thank you enough for all you have done for my family. You were there for them when I wasn't." He hung his head and wept as he spluttered, "I am so sorry for the way I treated you, you didn't deserve it."

Mother Squirrel's eyes grew wider in her head with shock and disbelief. She didn't recognise the man who stood in front of her. This wasn't the crazy monster she'd lived with for the last year. There were glimpses of the Squirrel she'd fallen in love with. She knew somewhere she still loved him, but it was going to take time to rebuild the trust he had broken between them.

Sensing it was time for them to leave, Brazil and his mother said, "We'll be off."

"Stop, please," Father Squirrel begged, "how can I make it right with you, with all the newcomers? I did such terrible things."

"Time," Brazil's Mother said wisely, "give them time, and if you are truly sorry, your actions will show them how you feel."

CHAPTER 44

The Fall of Monty

As spring turned to summer, the creatures of the Great Garden worked hard to make it up to the newcomers. Monty was delighted with their progress, and when it had come time for them to return to Manor Farm, it had been decided unanimously that they would all stay.

Summer was Monty's favorite time of year, and this was a particularly good one. From high in the Douglas Fir, he watched Spud tumbling around the great lawn with her seven babies and the Foxes, now proud grandparents, overlooking their brood. He smiled to himself as Narsus strutted down the gravel path followed by the three peahens and a string of fluffy chicks. Then Monty's heart swelled watching a very proud Father Squirrel patiently teach Hazel and Brazil's children how to climb a tree below.

Wriggling his stiff muscles Monty figured he'd sat for too long delighting in the new arrivals. He was used to his dreaded aches and pains, but today they were particularly bad. Added to this pain, his stomach churned, and his head was dizzy, but he ignored all of it, his focus was sounding the morning alert. He figured once he got the wind beneath his wings all would sort itself out as it usually did.

Steadying on the edge of his nest, he launched into flight. Just as he reached the point of no return when his huge wings opened to scoop the air beneath him, a pain seared through his body, leaving his wings jammed to his side. He tried desperately to move his wings, but his body wouldn't obey. The pain was agonising and the realisation of the earth rushing towards him at terrifying speeds caused him to cry out just as he hit the middle of the Great Lawn with a sickening thud.

There was a moment of silence in the garden as the creatures absorbed what had just happened. They stood like statues, frozen to the spot in disbelief, unable to move, paralyses with fear. Then as if the spell broke, a synchronised panic broke out as they all rushed together towards Monty's motionless body, screaming and crying hysterically.

CHAPTER 45

Ed to the Rescue

One of Ed's duties as head gardener was to open and lock up the gardens every day. The other gardeners joked that you could set your watch by him. He had worked man and boy in the gardens except for two weeks every autumn when he was made to visit his in-laws. His wife joked he might as well move into his potting shed because he spent so much time in it, and at times, Ed felt that wasn't a bad idea.

He realised something was wrong when he went to unlock the gate and neither the Raven nor the Heron were there to ignore him. His feeling of apprehension grew as he walked through the deserted visitors center and past the terrace with its swirling patterns of hundreds of brightly coloured flowers between perfectly trimmed box hedges.

Stopping to dead head, a flower, he was puzzled as he noticed the eerie silence in the garden. Looking down the gravel path towards the round pond to savor the magnificent view over the Long Water he gasped at the sight of hundreds of creatures in the middle of the Great Lawn under the Douglas Fir.

He stood for a moment in disbelief, never had he seen such a sight. He'd no idea that so many creatures lived in the Great Garden. He'd seen some of them over the years, but to see them all together in a mass was overwhelming. Slowly he inched closer. Something was wrong with the picture in front of him, Foxes stood amongst Rabbits and Geese. As he crept forward, he anticipated a mass dispersal at any second, but they sat there motionless like garden ornaments.

Following their gaze Monty's lifeless body came into sight and Ed slowly pulled his cap from his head and held it into his chest in respect for the old Bird. He stood with the lifeless creatures for serval minutes questioning if he was dreaming this. Then, a loud bang from a distant door broke the creature's trance. The creature's eyes flickered furtively scanning for danger, then Father Fox spotted Ed inches behind him and yelped, "Human!"

Instantly, Frogs jumped into the air as Rabbits leapt across their flight path colliding then all landing in heaps on the floor. Geese ran around and around in circles followed by their young unable to decide which way to run. Hedgehogs curled into balls and rolled across the lawn, picking up fallen leaves on the sharp prickles and squirrels darted up the Douglas Fir so quickly the causing its giant to rain down on Edd and Monty's motionless body.

Ed's arms instinctively flew to his head, and he dropped to the ground in a bid to protect himself. When the thudding finally stopped, he slowly lowered his arms and stood up questioning himself. Did that really happen? He thought nobody would believe what he'd just witnessed.

Looking around, he saw Monty's lifeless body lying on the floor. Well, that much was true, he reassured himself. Moving closer, he gently scooped Monty up and nestled him in his cap, "What happened to you, you poor old thing?" he asked Monty's lifeless body. Then suddenly he ran up the gravel path in the direction of his potting shed whilst the creatures peered from their hiding places in horror.

CHAPTER 46

In the Potting shed

Ed gently lay Monty on his workbench and prayed the old Raven was still alive, but he didn't hold out much hope. Carefully lifting Monty's body out of his cap, he could feel the warmth and dared to hope that he might still be alive. He'd grown fond of this old Bird. Trying to work out what to do, Ed was startled when his shed door flew open.

"Boss!" one of the young gardeners called excitedly.

"Not now Matt," Ed replied without looking up, "I have my hands full here."

"You have to see this," Matt said gesturing his arm, inviting Ed outside.

"I don't have to see anything," Ed said irritably staring at Monty not sure what to do.

"No really, Boss! You need to see this!" Matt insisted. Reluctantly leaving Monty, Ed stepped out into the sunshine, and his mouth fell open.

Perched high in perfect rows crowning the tall walls surrounding the kitchen garden sat every conceivable Bird: Ducks, Geese, Robins, Finches, Wrens, Blackbirds, Crows Sparrows, Swifts, Pigeons, Starlings, Magpies, Jays, Peacocks, Woodpeckers, and a loan Heron. Even the elusive Kingfishers they had heard of but had never seen stared down on him. Peppered between the Birds, he spotted Grey and Red Squirrels, Mice, and Frogs, and he wondered how on earth they got up there. Lowering his gaze through the open garden gate, he could see a mass of Rabbits, Badgers, Foxes, and even Rats looking pleadingly at him. He stood in stunned silence, mesmerised by the hypnotic constantly changing patterns of the sea of colourful Butterflies and Dragonflies.

Feeling the massive weight of responsibility, Ed knew they needed professional help. He ran back to Monty and gently wrapped him in a clean rag. Then, he shouted to Matt, "Get my keys, you're driving." And as he ran to his car, Ed said under his breath to the buddle in his arms, "You'd better stay with me or that lot will make my life hell."

The creatures watched in horror as they sped off down the drive. Where was that human taking their Monty? Why did he not just return him to them? Reluctantly the creatures returned to their homes to mourn their dear friend, hero, and guardian.

CHAPTER 47

Later that day

Monty slowly opened one eye after being aroused by muffled noises in the distance. His brain tried to identify the source of the noise as he fought to focus. He shook his head repeatedly in a bid to clear his vision as a vivid memory of the ground rushing up to meet him flooded his mind. He wondered if he was dead.

Bit by bit, he tried to make sense of his surroundings. He tried to move his wings, but they were tightly bound to his body with a piece of cloth. As his senses slowly returned, the sound of human voices close by sent his heart racing. Shaking his head again his vision started to clear and to his horror Lily smiled at him through the bars of a cage. "Welcome back, Monty. We get to fight another day," she purred delightedly.

Monty screeched in horror as the shed door flew open and Ed appeared. Sighing with relief he exclaimed "So you're awake!" He walked over to the cage and continued, "Thank God! You had us worried." Then realising Lily's presence was distressing Monty, Ed looked at Lily and said, "Out you go!" Then, seeing her resistance, he added, "Shoo! He needs all the rest he can get." Reluctantly, Lily obeyed, meowing over her shoulder, "You wait," she taunted, "I'll be back tonight when all the humans have gone."

With the door firmly closed behind her, Ed opened the cage door and Monty looked in terror as Ed's huge earth-encrusted hands came towards him. Monty's only defense was to jab at Ed's hands with his beak.

"Glad to see there's still some fight in you," Ed said, laughing at Monty's futile attack as he gently unbound his wings, freeing him in the cage.

"You had us all worried, the vet thinks you were poisoned." Then, Ed hung his head in shame. "I'm so sorry one of my new lads was sprayed weed killer on the East side of the garden." Then, he paused. "We had no idea how toxic the stuff was. I promise we will never use anything like that again." Ed stared into Monty's eyes, and somehow Monty knew he meant it. "Maybe we could make that bit of a wild meadow more suitable for you and your friends to live. Maybe you could get your friends to manage it for us?" He chuckled.

Then, as he walked to the door, he said back to him, "I'll let you rest. You'll need lots of that over the next few days to make you better." And he closed the door firmly behind him.

Monty stood in his cage, head tilted to one side, wondering what had just happened. He still wasn't sure if he was alive or dead. He puzzled, a human apologising to him. He'd never heard such a thing. Despite his best efforts to stay awake he fell back sleep.

CHAPTER 48

That Evening

Lily headed straight for the garden and hid. It was nearly closing time, and she knew the creatures would soon come out of hiding. Hearing Horus's signal, she watched as the creatures of the Great Garden and the newcomers united with grief gathered in the amphitheater.

Getting straight down to business, Father Fox took the lead. "I say we all go to the Kitchen Garden and dig up everything," he boomed in rage, and militant cheers went up.

"We can help!" shouted the Mice. "We can dig down and damage all the root veg."

"Please!" Horus pleaded. "Monty wouldn't want this."

"But he's not here, and the humans must pay," Father Fox shouted back at him to great cheers.

"Right," Father Fox said driving the rebellion forward, "from there, we will go to the ornamental gardens."

"What about the greenhouses?" Spud shouted. "I can take care of them, but I might need some help."

Father Fox nodded in agreement "You do that, and Birds go with her, you can go for any hanging fruits she can't reach. And Badgers, you take on the flower beds, moles you dig up the lawns. Nothing is to be left standing, is that clear!" he roared. The air was charged with venom as chants of "Humans must pay!" went up from the crowd.

Not able to listen to anymore, Lily sprang from her hiding place screaming, "Stop!" Instantly, mother creatures grabbed their babies ready to run, and father creatures jumped forward, teeth and claws out ready to attack.

"Stop!" Horus screamed, and they all froze. Moving closer, Horus asked Lilly, "What do you want?"

"You have it all wrong!" Lily pleaded. "Monty is alive!" The creatures, still poised for attack, circled her.

"How dare you!" Father Fox purred menacingly in her face. "How dare you come here saying such things?"

"Let her speak," Horus said taking control. "Let her speak!"

"It's true," Lily said, swallowing down her fear. "Ed took him to his friend a vet , and he fixed him."

Father Fox's nose pressed up against hers, and it was barely audible when she gulped loudly saying, "I can prove it. Come with me," she said as she turned, relieved to be moving away from Father Fox and she ran up the tree-lined avenue towards the big house with all the creatures in hot pursuit.

Lily ran ahead through an open gate the gardeners had forgotten to close. Reaching it Horus shouted, "Stop! This could be a trap!" He flapped his large wings and said moving forward, "Ok, I'll take it from here." And he moved forward towards Lily sitting outside Ed's potting shed in the far corner of the garden. Slowly, he inched forward, constantly scanning for danger. The creatures peered through the gateway and held their breath with the only sound being the rhythmic knocking of Horus' knees.

Reaching the window of the potting shed, Horus stood tall and peered in. Silent bittersweet tears rolled down his feathered face and dripped off his long beak. He was overjoyed to see his friend alive but saddened to see him in a cage.

Impatiently, Father Fox called to him, "Well, what can you see?" Horus croaked, "He's alive." Gasps of shock rippled through the creatures as the news registered.

"But how will we get him out of there?" Horus asked Lily.

"That's no problem," Lily offered. Calling to Spud and Father Fox, she instructed, "You two, come here." Spud bounced forward, delighted to be of service, but Grandpa Rabbit pulled at her tail and said, "Stop! How do you know she won't eat you?"

Lily laughed, "Will you lot get over yourself? Ed keeps me well-fed. Why would I be interested in eating one of you smelly creatures?"

"Don't worry," Mother Fox said bending down to Grandpa Rabbit. "Father Fox will look after her."

CHAPTER 49

Freeing Monty

Monty woke shivering with the memory of the terrible dream where he'd been trapped in a cage. As his eyes slowly focused, he realised it had not been a dream. Peering out of the dirty window, he could see the sun low in the sky and remembered Lily's words just as she shot through her cat flap and pounced onto the counter to peer in at him. Unable to help herself, she purred with delight seeing him there so vulnerable.

Outside, Father Fox rose onto his back legs and skillfully caught the shiny chrome handle and pulled it down causing the door to fly open. Quickly entering the shed, Spud leapt onto Father Fox's back and then up onto the workbench.

"Don't worry, Monty. We'll have you out of here in a jiffy." Spud said confidently but Monty didn't reply; he couldn't take his blurry eyes off Lily. Quickly Spud chewed at the piece of rope that kept Monty's cage door shut. When the rope finally fell to the floor, Lily hooked her paw around the door and pulled with all her might. With encouragement from all the cheering outside, she continued to pull at the door until finally it gave way and swung wide open, and Monty was free.

A huge roar of delight filled the kitchen garden when Father Fox appeared with a very fragile Monty clinging to his back. The creatures cheered and whooped as they processioned him home, delighted to have their leader back.

Horus stood at the back of the crowd silently watching the scene. Turning to Lily and said emotionally, "How can we ever thank you?" She purred sweetly at him, "I think it's time we stopped fighting, don't you?"

He smiled at her and said, "I do."

"Well, if you all keep out of the gardeners' way, I'll keep out of yours. How does that sound?"

"Sounds perfect to me," Horus nodded in agreement.

"Oh! And I wouldn't mind an invite to your Harvest Party," she cheekily added.

"Done!" Horus confirmed. "And you will always be welcome, to join us at the evening meeting too." Lily purred loudly; she was delighted to finally be one of the creatures from the Great Garden.

Reaching the gravel path that led to the Douglas Fir, Monty said to Father Fox, "Thank you, my friend. I've got it from here." As Father Fox carefully knelt, Monty slid off his back onto the path. As Monty's vision rectified itself, he felt like he was really seeing the garden for the first time. He marveled as sunlight bounced off the puddles and sunbeams peeped from behind the open gate. He could smell the beautiful heady scent of roses filling the air with a sweet background fragrance of honeysuckle. He stopped to take a drink from a fresh puddle, and for the first time, he could taste the deliciousness of rainwater—its freshness, the feel of it on his beak, the cooling sensation as it trickled down his throat and dripped off his feathers. Behind the cheers and encouragement from the creatures, he could hear the distant metal Bird that flew through the sky. He could hear a squeaking hinge of a gate in need of oil as it moved in the breeze, the crunch of the gravel beneath his feet as he walked. He had never experienced a garden like this. He marveled at the colours of the trees, the textures of their trunks, and how there were so many different types. He had never realised the differing shapes and sizes of leaves. He realised he had taken all of this for granted.

CHAPTER 50

The Next Morning

Pulling up for work the next day, Ed was mystified to see both Horus and Monty perched high on the gate, welcoming him. Getting out of his car, he stood for a moment staring at the old Bird. "Well, I'll be!" he said pulling off his cap and scratching his head. "How did you get out? And look at you up there!" then turning his attention to Horus, "Just you remember the vet said he needs lots of rest." Looking back at Monty he said, "And you, look after yourself." and for the first time, Monty looked back at him. He really looked at him and had the realisation that not all Humans were bad. He beamed love and gratitude towards Ed for saving his life. Taking his unspoken cue, Ed replied, "You're welcome. Now, go check your kingdom and remember to rest. Let your big pal there take the burden."

Monty did as Ed advised and went back to his nest.

Delighted with Monty's miraculous recovery, the residents of the Great Garden respected his request for solitude. They regularly checked in on him. They took turns bringing him food, but they never disturbed his recuperation.

As the days passed and his body grew stronger, his mind grew more troubled. What if he had got it all wrong? He replayed it over and over in his brain. All his life he had hated all humans because of the unkind acts of a few. But Ed had proven they were capable of love and kindness. He had also judged the Rats and Minks the same, yet Mother Rat had proven she could be the perfect mother and resident. He had even misjudged Lily, she just wanted to feel like she belonged.

He knew his days in the garden were numbered as his cycle of life was drawing to a close. He wasn't sad; he knew for every beautiful new arrival, a creature had to depart. It was simple, and he doubted he would survive another winter. But he had been given a second chance, a wake-up call, and he wanted to make the most of it. He'd seen his life's work was flawed, and he wondered if he had enough time to put it right.

He'd cursed himself for being so focused on the creatures in the Garden, keeping them safe, ensuring harmony living a good life, but there was a big world out there, and he wanted the same dream for every creature on the planet.

CHAPTER 51

Summer Unfolds

Taking a well-earned break from teaching his grandchildren to climb, Father Squirrel sat high in a birch tree and smiled as he watched them play. Brazil climbed up beside him with the same look of love and pride all over his face.

"They really are something special," Father Squirrel said with pure adoration.

"They sure are, but we are biased," Brazil agreed smiling.

Then, changing the subject, Father Squirrel asked, "How bad is it over there?"

"Over where?" Brazil said confused.

"Manor Farm, I mean how dangerous is it?"

"Why?" Brazil said smiling. "Do you want us to go back?"

"Not a chance!" Father Squirrel said firmly. "I couldn't bear to be separated from you all now. No, it's just, I can't explain it, but I have this nagging feeling that I need to go there. Maybe it's to understand what life outside this garden is really like."

"I would offer to go with you, but to be honest, I never want to see that place again," Brazil said remembering how tough it was.

"I wouldn't ask you, son, your place is here looking after this lot," he said as he smiled and turned to watch his grandchildren happily playing.

CHAPTER 52

Father Squirrel visits Manor Farm

Early the next morning, Father Squirrel said a tearful goodbye to Mother Squirrel. "Don't worry love, I promise I will be home before dark tonight".

"You'd better be," she replied as she watched him climb down the riverbank and jump onto his friend Father Otter's back. As they silently glided through the water, Father Squirrel questioned his own sanity.

"He'll be ok," Brazil said putting an arm around Mother Squirrel. He didn't understand why Father Squirrel needed to go, but he couldn't talk him out of it.

"Thanks mate," Father Squirrel said to his friend when they reached the other side of the river.

"Are you sure you want to do this?" Father Otter questioned again.

Father Squirrel nodded, then turned to climb the steep riverbank.

"Shall I wait for you?" Father Otter offered.

"No, I'll be ok. I'll give you a shout when I'm ready," Father Squirrel replied.

Reaching the top of the riverbank, Father Squirrel was amazed at how quickly Mother Nature repaired itself. The scorched bank and charred field were lush green again. He watched in wonder at the patterns the wind made on the swaying field of corn. He wished it could all be that simple for him, but he knew he had brought huge pain to a lot of creatures, and it wasn't going to be an easy road back. Lost in his thoughts, he was unaware of the young Hawk overhead. Suddenly spotting him, Father Squirrel jumped up the nearest tree just as the farm Cat pounced and landed where he had been standing a fraction of a second earlier. Shaken, Father Squirrel ran for his life hearing someone behind him.

"He was mine," the Cat screamed at the Hawk.

"You're too fat and too slow," laughed the Hawk.

Father Squirrel surveyed the landscape. This place was so different from the lush forest garden of Wrest Park. There were no trees to swing from, just endless open space framed with a fine line of bushes and dotted with the odd tree. Again, he questioned himself, why had he come? He looked back at the river as fear encouraged him to go home, but Father Otter had already disappeared out of sight.

Closely watching the Hawk circling above him, Father Squirrel heard him gibe the Cat, "You had your chance, now watch an expert in action." As he skillfully swooped in to pick Father Squirrel from the branch.

Not prepared to be either creature's lunch, Father Squirrel bit into the branch he was clinging to then jumped to another. As the Hawk flew in with feet outstretched, Father Squirrel let go of the branch in his mouth catapulting it at the Hawk. The branch delivered a mighty smack on the Bird's backside. The Hawk whooped in pain as it fought to regain its flight path and the Cat rolled around howling with laughter. Seizing his chance, Father Squirrel shot down the tree and disappeared into a nearby hedge.

Shaking in the bush, Father Squirrel knew his best chance of safety was to get to the next tree. Jumping from bush to bush, he became aware of red fur close to him, that wasn't his own. "You're a long way from home," a Fox said, licking his lips as it ran alongside him. Reaching a tree, Father Squirrel shot up to its tallest branch.

"He's mine," screamed the Hawk as he dove down a second time just missing Father Squirrel who jumped to a lower branch only to find the Cat climbing the tree below him. Furious he might miss out on a meal, the Fox bit into the Cat's tail and pulled hard. "What are you doing?" screamed the Cat.

"He's mine," the Fox said menacingly. "I've never eaten a red one!"

As the Fox and Cat fought, Father Squirrel dove into the thick green field of corn. Oh, how he wished he'd never come as he was forced further away from the river, safety and home.

Entering the lush green corn, Father Squirrel looked up at the sky, visible through dozens of spider webs glistening in the summer sun. With no sign of the Hawk above, he scanned the long corridors between the corn for the Cat and the Fox. Afraid to stop, he started running until he sensed the ground shuddering beneath his feet. Then forced to duck he curled into a tiny ball as a family of Rabbits leapt over his head screaming "run, the poisonous gas is coming". Father Squirrel had no idea what they were talking about but as he lay there, the rumble grew even stronger.

Jumping to his feet, he ran further into the field crashed into a sea of Crickets jumping through the air. Changing directions, he nearly passes out as a huge Grass Snake shot towards him. Closing his eyes, convinced he was the Snake's dinner, the smelly rain started to fall like a fine mist taking his breath away. As his cough grew stronger so did his need for air and his head spiraled until finally everything went blank, and he collapsed on the ground as huge black tires skimmed his motionless tiny body.

CHAPTER 53

Mother Squirrel Waits

Mother Squirrel paced up and down the riverbanks. Her stomach was whirling around with a bad feeling. She didn't understand why Father Squirrel had gone to Manor Farm. She had begged him not to, but he'd insisted he had to do it. She wondered if he was punishing himself for what he'd done. She tried to concentrate on her breathing to calm herself down, but it was no use. She thought of how well he had done turning his life around and how hard he had worked to make it up to everyone. Since waking from his winter sleep, he'd found and mended a new home for the Grey Squirrels close to their own. He'd fetched and carried all the food Mother Rat and her brood could possibly eat. He'd carried out every task the creatures asked of him, including climbing into Father Fox's mouth when he got a thorn stuck in his tongue. He had worked day and night to make amends, so she was confused why he had insisted on going to the Farm.

Spinning around sensing somebody behind her, she found Mother Hedgehog.

"Would you like some company?" Mother Hedgehog softly said, her misery evident in her voice.

Nodding, Mother Squirrel sat down and patted the grass beside her. Mother Hedgehog sat in silence as the two creatures watched and willed Father Squirrel's safe return.

CHAPTER 54

Father Squirrel Saved

Father Squirrel opened his eyes; instinctively, he knew he was deep underground. "Where am I?" he coughed repeatedly as a Hedgehog came into focus.

"Are you feeling better?" the Hedgehog enquired, offering him some water cupped in a leaf.

Rubbing his head, Father Squirrel said, "What happened?"

"I found you passed out," he said, encouraging, "drink the water. It's fresh."

Overcome by the first kindness he had been shown since his arrival at Manor Farm, Father Squirrel gratefully gulped down the cool water.

"You're not from around here," the Hedgehog said.

"Why because of the colour of my fur?" Father Squirrel asked.

"No, the fact you didn't know to get below ground when humans were spraying their poison."

"I'm from across the river," he said between gulps. "And I need to get back to my family. They will be worried. What time is it?" he asked.

"Oh, I'd say must be 10 by now," the Hedgehog replied.

"Ten in the morning?" Father Squirrel asked.

The Hedgehog roared laughing, "Ten at night. You slept all day."

"What?!" Father Squirrel jumped up in a panic. "Mother Squirrel will be frantic. I promised I'd be home early."

A silent tear ran down the hedgehog's face. "It's been a long time since someone missed me."

"Do you have a family?" Father Squirrel enquired.

"Once, before the fire came," he said, wiping the tears from his face with his paw. Then, he continued, "Now, they're all gone."

Slowing down in respect of the poor Hedgehog's misery, Father Squirrel said, "I'm so sorry to hear that. But I must get home."

Father Hedgehog jumped into action, "We will need to be quick and get you to the river before the greedy Owl wakes." He ran out of the burrow, and Father Squirrel followed. At the water's edge, Father Squirrel let out a cry to signal for Father Otter to come for him.

CHAPTER 55

Out of the mist

Hearing Father Squirrel's call, Mother Squirrel jumped to her feet as Father Otter flew past her. Curious to see what all the excitement was about, the other creatures gathered. "It's him," Mother Squirrel wept and flung her arms around Mother Hedgehog. "He's safe."

On the other side of the riverbank, Father Squirrel and the Hedgehog hid in the reads as it darkened and the chances of the Owl being out with her insatiable appetite grew higher.

"Will you be all right to get home?" Father Squirrel asked the Hedgehog.

"Don't worry about me lad, you just get back safe to your family."

Then, they both jumped when Father Otter's head popped out of the water.

"Am I glad to see you!" he said to Father Squirrel.

"Not as glad as I am to see you," he smiled back.

"Who's your friend?" Father Otter enquired.

Father Squirrel looked at the Hedgehog, "You saved my life, and I don't even know your name." but before he had chance to answer the three creatures leapt as a loud hoot came from behind them.

Slowly turning, they saw two huge eyes staring back at them, "Well, what have we here?" she hooted again. "A three-course meal, I fancy." She tilted her head and began deciding whom she was going to eat first.

Grabbing the Squirrel and Hedgehog's hands, Father Otter dove backwards into the water, dragging them after him.

Bobbing to the surface in the thick mist that hung over the river, Father Otter said to the Hedgehog, "She will not find us in here. I can drop you off further up the riverbank where you will be safe."

"Why don't you come with us?" Father Squirrel suggested to the Hedgehog, then sensing his hesitation, added, "What have you to go back to? At least you will be safe in the garden."

Agreeing with a nod, the three creatures made their way across the river.

Mother Squirrel sat in silence in a huddle with her family staring into the mist wishing Father Squirrel home. Around them sat neat rows of Geese, Rabbits, Peacocks, Frogs, and Toads. They were now being joined by the Badgers and Foxes who were awakening from their sleep. The branches in the nearby tree bowed with a Birds who sat frustrated unable to help. They had tried to search for Father Squirrel, but visibility was so poor they were forced to sit and wait with everyone else.

Mother Squirrel was unusually still, hardly taking a breath. Then through the silence came the call from Father Squirrel and the instant splash of Father Otter going to his rescue.

"He's safe!" Mother Squirrel cried as she ran closer to the water's edge. She could hear the sound of splashing and voices as it gradually got louder.

"Is that really you?" Mother Squirrel was desperate for reassurance.

"It is me my love! "We are nearly there," Father Squirrel shouted back.

Father Squirrel gradually appeared through the white curtain of fog Father Fox jumped into the water and flung a heavy, wet Father Squirrel onto his shoulders and triumphantly paraded him up and down the riverbank to the cheers of the crowd before placing him gently beside Mother Squirrel.

Tears of gratitude rolled down Mother Squirrel's face as she embraced him, and another big cheer went up from all the creatures celebrating Father Squirrel's safe return.

"I'm so sorry my love," Father Squirrel cried repeatedly. "I got into a bit of trouble, and my good friend here saved me." The creatures followed his gaze to see another creature coming out of the fog. Overexcited, Father Fox bounded down the riverbank and grabbed the Hedgehog in his mouth. Seeing the gleaming white fangs coming in his direction, the Hedgehog sprang into a tight ball just as Father Fox closed his mouth.

Yelping in pain, Father Fox forcefully expelled the Hedgehog, sending the prickly ball flying through the air and landing in the middle of the onlookers. Slowly uncurling, the Hedgehog took in his new surroundings, then he fixated on something, and they all followed his stare. "Is it really you?" he choked, looking at Mother Hedgehog. Then suddenly, it made sense when Maisie and her brother Corny ran towards them screaming Papa.

CHAPTER 56

Monty's appearance

The creatures were surprised and delighted when Monty flew in for the evening meeting. Scanning the crowd, his heart warmed to see the way the creatures had welcomed Lily. He was impressed with Horus' leadership and the way he conducted the meeting and delegated jobs for the upcoming Harvest celebration. When Horus announced any more business, Monty hobbled forward to take his place in front of them.

"As you know, I've been unwell," he started, "and I thank you all for your good wishes and for respecting my need for space. I've spent my time reflecting and contemplating my life. I have something I feel is very important to share with you." The crowd was silent. "As you all know, we live in this amazing place," he held out his wing and slowly looked all around him. "But it is not just the surroundings, beautiful as they are, it is you that make this a magical place to live. It's the way you look out for each other. The love and kindness you demonstrate when one of you is in need. I'm so proud to have been part of all this." He took a minute to look each creature in the eye.

They could see he had changed. He wasn't Monty the Boss you dare not cross, the rule maker and upholder of the peace. He looked so fully alive. His body was old and battered, but vitality shone from his eyes, and they craved that sense of peace. "I've realised this shouldn't be unique to our garden. What if everybody got to live in a world like this?"

"But how?" Mother Fox questioned gently.

He smiled and answered, "I've spent weeks considering this. I look upon every one of you as family. We are all different, unique and at the same time, we all want to love and be loved. Yes, things happen to us along the way that leave us angry, frustrated, even fearful, but they are lessons we can either learn from and move on, or we stay stuck living with bitterness and hatred all our lives. It is our choice."

He looked at Father Squirrel with his shiny red coat and plump cheeks, happily surrounded by his loving family. He stood with one of Hazel and Brazil's beautiful babies in one arm and his other firmly around Mother Squirrel. Father Squirrel smiled a grateful smile back at him and stepped forward.

"You're right," he said looking at some of the newcomers, "I will never be able to make it up to you. I had no idea what you were suffering from. I grew up in this world of privilege, and I took it all for granted. After visiting your old world, I am even more ashamed of how I treated you. If it wasn't for," and he pointed to Father Hedgehog, "one creature's kindness, I wouldn't be here now."

"I know this won't be an overnight thing," Monty continued, "but imagine the rewards."

"But where do we start?" Father Badger asked, overwhelmed by the idea.

"I suggest you start close to home. Love and cherish yourselves and your families and each other, then move it out. Look for love in every creature you meet on your journey, no matter what their species or how they choose to live their lives. Migrating Birds, when you go on your travels, greet every creature you meet as if they were a resident of this garden. Look for the love and the good in them."

There was a long silence as they all soaked up his wisdom.

Eventually, Mother Rat said very timidly, "What about the Rats and Minks from the swamp?" Instantly, the atmosphere changed, and muttering started.

"Especially them," Monty replied cheerily. "They need our love and help more than anybody."

"But we can't trust them!" stated Mother Fox.

"That is what we believed, but Mother Rat here has proven there is good in every species."

Mother Rat sat proudly in front of them with her 10 impeccably behaved children. "They're not all bad, they just haven't been shown the way," Mother Rat added. "They have the same hopes and dreams you have for your children; they just don't know how to change."

After another long silence, then Father Squirrel said softly, "So how do we move forward?"

Monty suggested, "Maybe we can invite them to our Harvest Celebration party?"

"But what about their crazy partying ways?" Mother Squirrel said in panic, terrified they would tempt Father Squirrel back into his bad habits. Father Squirrel pulled her closer to reassure her that was never going to happen again. He was so grateful to have his family back and being a grandfather was the best experience of his life; he was determined never to mess that up again.

"We could make it clear with our invitation," Horus said calmly. "Let them know it's time to celebrate, give thanks, have fun but not go too wild."

Monty smiled; Horus was going to be a great leader.

CHAPTER 57

We Come in Peace

It was agreed upon to invite the Minks and Rats to the Harvest Party. Father Fox and Badger were given the task of asking them, and as they climbed under the fallen tree entering the swamp, Father Fox announced their arrival with a long, shaky howl. As their eyes adjusted to the shadowy light, they realised they were surrounded. Large logs were positioned on the sloping banks above them with Rats waiting for the command to set them flying whilst Minks hung from branches overhead cradling rocks, itching to let them go.

"We come in peace," Father Badger stuttered as Morris the head Mink charged at them. Pushing his face up against Father Badger's, Father Badger gazed into Morris' battle-scarred face and tried to ignore the sour smell of his breath. "Look for the love," he repeated in his head.

"We'd like to invite you to our Harvest Party," Father Fox quivered.

"You what?" Morris stood on his hind legs to get nose to nose with Father Fox.

Morris mimicked Father Fox, "We'd like to invite you to our Hhhhharvest Party." Then, he fell to the floor laughing and a terrifying cackle of laughter echoed up from the swamp.

Father Badger looked at Father Fox and willed him to keep looking at Morris with love. This was the hardest thing Father Fox had ever done. Standing there, letting them humiliate him was agonising. Fighting to ignore the voice in his head that screamed, "Are you going to let him speak to you like that? Go on taking him out and the others will fall into line." When he didn't respond, the voice shouted louder, "Go on, one bite and this nasty piece of work will be gone." But Father Fox told the voice to shut up, he took deep breaths and calmly looked Morris the Mink in the eye and replied levelly, "Yes, we would like you to come." The other Rats and Minks went silent, confused at the invitation.

"It's a trap!" Morris shouted.

"No," Father Badger said quietly. "We'd like to make amends. We want to say sorry for fighting with you."

Morris glared at Father Badger, "Oh you would, would you? Do you think we're fools?"

"No!" said Father Fox. "We were out of order fighting with you, and we want to make up for it." He slowly turned to the crowd to look each one in the eye, hoping to convince them they were sincere. "The creatures of the Great Garden would be honored if you would join us to give thanks for Mother Nature's bounty. Please bring your families. It will be a night of good food, fun, and celebration." Then, sensing the atmosphere in the swamp relax a little, they decided it was time to retreat.

Just as they were about to squeeze under the fallen tree, Morris the Mink shouted, "Don't forget that young Rabbit promised us tomatoes."

CHAPTER 58

The Evening Meeting

Eagerly waiting for news of Father Fox and Badger's mission, the creatures gathered for their evening meeting. They were relieved to see their return when they ran into the amphitheater and dramatically collapsed in the middle. All the creatures rushed around to see if they were alright.

"Did they hurt you?" Mother Fox fussed over Father Fox, and he lapped it up.

"What did they say?" Father Hedgehog asked eagerly.

"What did they do?" Mother Goose followed.

Father Fox opened his mouth to recount their experience, but Monty threw open his wings to silence him. He only wanted facts not details that might feed the prejudice against the swamp creatures further. Moving closer to Father Badger and Fox, he shooed the other creatures back to their places, then asked, "Are they coming?"

"We think so," Father Badger said, "if we have tomatoes."

"Oh no," Lily jumped forward, "Ed would be very upset if you stole his tomatoes."

"You're right," Monty agreed, "but if that's what they want, then somehow, that's what we need to get."

Lily started to protest, but Monty raised his wing and commanded silence. Then, turning his attention, he requested, "I need you all to close your eyes." The creatures all complied except Lily. "Please," Monty encouraged her. Closing his own eyes, he continued, "Imagine tomatoes, big ripe juicy tomatoes. Picture them in the middle of our feast and think about how excited you will feel seeing them there. Remember how delicious they taste and smell. Imagine yourself biting into one—the sweetness of the juice running down your throat. Don't think about how we are going to get them, just imagine having them there with all our new swamp friends happily enjoying them with us."

CHAPTER 59

The Day of the Harvest Party

Ed really enjoyed his morning and evening chats with Monty. A real bond had grown between them even though they had no common language, but a sense of true friendship united them both wanting the best for the garden and all who lived in it.

Locking up that night, a memory resurfaced in Ed's mind. Early one morning the same time the year before when he was patrolling the garden, he'd found a strange arrangement in the middle of the Great Lawn. At first, he thought it was just rubbish whipped up by the wind, but moving closer, he'd been surprised to find a carpet of wildflowers and leaves with masses of half-eaten seeds, nuts, and berries strewn across it. He'd laughed to himself thinking somebody must have had a good party and judging by all the lumps of red fur dancing around on the Autumn breeze, it must have ended up a wild one. Then, he busied himself clearing it up. Thinking over recent events, he wondered if he'd been right.

Snapping out of his thought, he said to himself, "You're starting to lose it, old man." But the thing that puzzled him the most was the naked tomato vines that sat pride of place in the middle of the carpet. Without questioning his actions, he went into the glass house and snipped the finest vine loaded with ripe tomatoes and popped them into a brown paper bag before continuing his rounds.

As Ed was about to close the main gate, he looked up at Monty and Horus and said, "I feel a bit daft." Taking off his cap and scratching his head, he said, "I don't know why, but I thought you lot might enjoy these." and he carefully placed the paper bag on the floor just inside the gate and closed it. Seeing the tomatoes peeping out of the bag Horus nearly fell from his perch in surprise as Monty looked at him smiling and said, "See, I knew it would sort itself."

CHAPTER 60

The Party

The creatures of the garden sat around the beautiful spread of food with the tomatoes center stage and waited for their guests. Mother Rat prayed they would come. It was over a year since she had seen her family, and she missed them terribly. Patiently, they sat on, and even though they were hungry, nobody wanted to start eating without their guests. As the darkness fell, they doubted the Swamp Creatures were coming.

Losing patience, Mother Rat jumped up ready to run in the direction of the swamp. "Stop!" Horus shouted after her. "Believe, and they will come."

"I can't," she said, turning back. "I know they're too scared of Morris!" Then biting off a ripe tomato, she ran in the direction of the swamp with it hanging from her mouth. Father Fox and Badger grabbed the rest of the tomatoes and followed her, yelling, "She could be right." All the creatures grabbed what they could carry and chased after them. At the fallen tree, Father Fox let out his howl, and instantly, hundreds of pairs of hungry eyes peered out of the gloom of the swamp.

"We've brought food" Mother Rat said holding up the tomato, "and she smiled when some of the eyes moved towards her. Then, Morris growled, "Stop! It's a trap."

"No, it's not," Mother Rat hollered back. Then, in a gentler voice, she said, "It's an opportunity. An opportunity to have the life you have dreamed of. These are good creatures. They helped me and my children, and they want to do the same for you. I know you are fed up with life in the swamp, fighting every day to survive. There's loads of room and food for you in the Great Garden, you just need to trust there is a better way."

The eyes slowly moved forward, then closer again, and then more eyes appeared in the darkness behind them. They all froze with another scream from Morris. "Stop!" he roared, sensing he was losing control. "They will make you weak!"

"No," Father Fox said, "we will help you get stronger; you just need to trust us."

"Trust you!" Morris roared a "ha, ha". "Remember what they did the last time they were all here."

"Yes, and we are truly sorry. We don't want to fight anymore, please let us make it up to you," Father Fox implored. Slowly, softly, the eyes moved forward until whole faces appeared in the twilight. Despite Morris's desperate cries "It's a trap!" The Rats and Minks continued to edge forward into the light until face to face they all stood looking into each other's faces. The creatures of the Great Garden were surprised at how different the swamp creatures looked. The battle scars on their faces seemed to fade when they smiled.

Holding out the food to their guests, Mother Rat said, "We figured if you wouldn't come to our party, we'd bring it to you." She handed her tomatoes to a couple of Minks who gladly accepted it.

At first, simple pleasantries were exchanged, like how delicious the tomatoes were. Then, more meaningful conversations began as slowly, the barriers came down with the sharing of food and laughter.

Monty watched the whole evening from a distance, delighted with the behavior and reaction of each creature as trust and friendship grew. Returning to the Great Garden they continued their celebrations, and the swamp creatures were invited to stay.

Monty thanked Mother Nature for the extra time she had given him and the chance to come back and put things right. Carefully, he took his very tired aching body home and fell into a deep, blissful, endless sleep.

Printed in Great Britain
by Amazon